Praise for
Living Outside the l

MW01093105

Individuals, communities, and governments are just starting to realize the impact electronic media have had on our health, values, and future. People want to retake control of their lives and establish bonds with family, friends, and neighbors. *Living Outside the Box* is an empowering example of what each one of us can do, for ourselves and for our families, by the following the examples set by those who have walked this path before us.

**—Robert Kesten, executive director,
Center for Screen-Time Awareness**

Family rituals can be either positive or negative. For too many families, TV watching has become a negative ritual. Barb Brock's thorough, compelling studies of families who tamed the tube (those who watch little or no TV) uncovered two startling facts: most people find it easier to quit TV than they expect, and they find the benefits of quitting to be far greater than imagined. If you think your family is watching too much TV, read this book! If you're going to a baby shower anytime soon, buy this book as a gift!

—Meg Cox, author of
***The Book of New Family Traditions:
How to Create Great Rituals for Holidays and Everyday***

As national coordinator of the nation-wide "Take Back Your Time" movement, I have been incredibly impressed by Barb Brock's research. I have heard her speak about gathering information from hundreds of TV-free families, and the results are astonishing. Though still very techno-savvy, this population of TV-free Americans made a choice that favors family and community—something we all might want to emulate. Taking back even half of our television time to get involved with good leisure would produce a much more vibrant and interesting society. All Americans, but especially those who have children, should read this book!

—John de Graaf, co-author of
Affluenza: The All-Consuming Epidemic

In April 2005 I visited Barbara Brock at her home near Spokane, Washington. I came under the banner of friendship, but to be honest I wanted to see if she practiced what she preached. Her house was full of beautiful homemade furnishings—furniture, quilts, and decorative accents. She prepared a meal for me, the contents of which came from the family garden. Her husband, Vern, and their two children, Sydney and Adam, joined us. We talked while we dined, and I learned of several additional projects in various stages of completion. It all seemed so civilized. After lunch, Barb and I strolled about the woods scattered throughout the property. All too soon, it was time for me to take my leave. As I drove down the narrow lane leading away from the Brock homestead, I kept asking myself, "Where do they find the time?" Then it dawned on me . . .

—Dan Dustin,
professor and chair,
Department of Parks, Recreation, and Tourism, University of Utah

living
outside
the BOX

eastern washington university press

living outside the BOX

tv-free families share their secrets

barbara brock

11 10 09 08 07   1 2 3 4 5

"The One-Eyed Monster, and Why I Don't Let Him In"
(copyright © 2002 by Barbara Kingsolver) originally
appeared in *Small Wonder: Essays by Barbara Kingsolver*,
pp. 131–43. Portions of the essay are reprinted here
by permission of HarperCollins Publishers.

Cover and interior design by A. E. Grey.

Cover images used by permission. Copyright Art Parts | Ron and Joe, Inc.

Library of Congress Cataloging-in-Publication Data

Brock, Barbara J. (Barbara Jean)
    Living outside the box : tv-free families share their secrets / Barbara Brock.
       p. cm.
    Includes bibliographical references.
    ISBN 1-59766-014-0
    1. Television and family. 2. Family recreation. 3. Television—
Psychological aspects.   I. Title.
   HQ520.B76 2006
   302.23'450973—dc22

                                                      2006016199

♾ The paper used in this publication meets the minimum
requirements of ANSI/NISO Z39.48-1992 (Permanence of Paper).

Eastern Washington University Press
Spokane and Cheney, Washington

To my husband, Vern, and our great kids,
Adam and Sydney, who pack our lives
with fun, music, adventure, and memories.
Not a day goes by when I am not grateful
for the TV-free decision that we
"accidentally" made twenty-two years ago.
And to my wonderfully creative parents,
Bob and Nadene Bryan, whose enthusiasm
for their seemingly endless hobbies has
been an inspiration.

contents

Foreword by Michael Gurian   ix

Acknowledgments   xi

Introduction: Out of the Closet   3

1: The Rise (and Fall) of Recreation   9

2: Fear of Leisure   17

3: A Word from Our Sponsors   27

4: How to Miss Nothing   39

5: The Decision to Go TV Free   49

6: Regarding Our Children   79

7: Thirty Days Without Television   99

8: Breaking the Soft Addiction   115

9: Voices of Experience   137

10: Time for Reflection   149

Appendix A
The TV-Free Survey   157

Appendix B
TV-Free Families in America   171

Appendix C
Exercises and Activities   185

Notes   197

Bibliography   207

About the Author   213

foreword

When I was young, I watched a black-and-white television with four stations: NBC, ABC, CBS, and PBS. Quite often, the antennae worked badly, and I sometimes stared at the "snow." I might have watched an hour of TV a day; the rest of my time was spent learning, playing outside, grabbing time with family and friends.

Things have changed for children. On average, our kids spend 900 hours a year in school but 1,023 hours watching TV. By the time our children reach the age of eighteen, they will have spent 22,000 hours watching TV—more time than they devote to any other activity besides sleeping. By age sixteen, they will have seen 200,000 acts of violence, 33,000 of them acts of murder. Two-thirds of preschoolers sit in front of screens for two or more hours each day—more than three times the hours they spend looking at books or being read to. Over half of children eight years and older have a TV in their bedroom, and 81 percent watch it alone and unsupervised.

Is this healthy? Are we, as parents, in control of the situation? Has television replaced "play"? These are big questions, and I have certainly faced them as a parent. Healthy brain development, social skills, conflict resolution, and creativity need outside time, free time, nonelectronic time. TV can be a good thing, but too much of it is dangerous to our loved ones.

In *Living Outside the Box*, Barbara Brock tackles the issue of television overuse head on and proposes a very simple, compelling, and manageable "magic bullet" solution. In the course of her research, she gathered data from twelve hundred TV-free men, women, and children across the country. These TV-free families have powerful and crucial things to teach all of us, especially those of us whose children do watch TV.

Living Outside the Box begins with the importance of quality leisure in our lives, contrasting recreational pursuits from the first half of the twentieth century, before the advent of television, with its present-day use. Brock includes the latest information on patterns of TV viewing, links our

TV habit to many other social movements and issues, including consumerism, and explains what "screen addiction" is.

One of the most powerful sections of the book involves the pilot study "30 Days Live." A group of fourth-, fifth-, and sixth-graders were asked to turn off *all* screens for a month. Their choice of foods and their level of physical activity were monitored. The improvements to these children's lives were nothing short of amazing. Physical, emotional, and ethical development flourished in ways that even the children's parents would not have imagined before the study.

Quite fascinating to me was that, while half the children predicted before the start of the study they wouldn't be able to last for a whole month without screen time, 77 percent of them succeeded—and many of these kids decided not to go back! They realized that life was best lived "outside the box." This came as little surprise to Brock, whose own household is TV-less. As she puts it, "My husband and I have raised a couple of normal, fun-loving kids in a TV-free home for twenty-two years amidst a gaggle of pets, hobbies, and fulfilling activities. Our kids thank us."

I have supported Brock's ideas for years and have drawn on her research in *The Minds of Boys* and *The Wonder of Girls*. Her approach is neither preachy nor melodramatic. She records many candid stories about TV-free existence and about the process of withdrawal from television, and then backs this anecdotal material up with evidence of the long-term benefits and life-changing effects of living without television. She shows why so many people discover a new life as they get control of the screen time in their homes—better marriages, fewer conflicts among siblings, healthier, better adjusted children.

This book is not just about television—it is about the health and happiness of our American population. To appreciate its wisdom, you do not need to begin by turning off your television altogether. But reading this book will help you to understand why this might be a good idea. *Living Outside the Box* will give you the inspiration and the tools you need to create a family and personal life in keeping with your own highest ideals.

—**Michael Gurian,**
Spokane, Washington, 2007

acknowledgments

To Henry Labalme, Frank Vespe, Robert Kesten, and the dedicated staff at the Center for Screen-Time Awareness in Washington, D.C., who were my sounding board and inspiration throughout the research.

To the awesome teachers who supported "30 Days Live" in their classrooms and the wonderful Eastern Washington University students who assisted with the research.

To Michael Gurian, steady supporter, whose insightful books and words made me realize the importance of telling stories about the TV-free choice.

To professors Tom Goodale, Dan Dustin, and Geof Godbey, who took the time to nurture a novice researcher and share their wisdom and ideas.

To Ann Ruethling, founder of Chinaberry, for putting me in touch with TV-free families from among her readership. And to Mary Pipher, who told me, "You write the book, and we'll change the world together."

To Robert Putnam and Robert Kubey, two brilliant researchers who are committed to educating others about the effects of screens on our lives and for whose unflagging support I will ever be grateful.

To Meg Cox, who gave me the courage to touch my toes in the icy waters of publishing.

To Claudia Wallis, of *Time* magazine, who was among the first in the media to take an interest in my research and wanted to let the world know about it. To Katie Couric, who invited me to New York for a thoughtful interview on the *Today Show* about the hundreds of TV-free families scattered across the country. And to all the newspapers and magazine writers who interviewed me about the lives of TV-free families. We had many a wonderful conversation, which left us all thinking that this world would be a great deal better off with less TV.

To Eastern Washington University, which has given me the chance to teach what I love for the past twenty years and granted me a sabbatical to conduct research and write about the TV families in this book. Each day I type the password "I Love EWU" on my laptop . . . and mean it. And to Eastern Washington University Press. When I first approached the Press and met the former assistant director, Scott Poole, who *loved* the idea ("So where's the goddamn TV?"), it felt like going home. Chris Howell, Ivar Nelson, and Steve Meyer, thank you for your support. And, especially, to Pamela Holway, my "ferocious" but extremely kind and talented editor: your commitment to this project has been a marvel.

And, above all, to the hundreds of TV-free families who trusted in a far-away, unknown professor, opened their hearts, and shared their wonderful, inspiring, funny, and memorable stories. I would *never* have written this book without your encouragement.

living
outside
the **BOX**

introduction:
out of the closet

This is a book about leisure. Specifically, it is about the importance of "good" leisure—recreational activities that allow us to unwind but at the same time demand a degree of mental and/or physical exertion. Paradoxical though it may seem, good leisure, even when it is physically tiring, leaves us energized. It is not only relaxing but revitalizing. Spending time on a hobby, getting some exercise, reading a good book or watching a film, having an extended conversation with a friend or family member, doing something creative, or even lying on the couch and focusing our attention on a piece of music—such recreational pursuits engage our minds (and possibly our bodies as well). And because they are in some measure stimulating, such activities provide more than relaxation: they generate a sense of satisfaction.

So what about television? Does watching TV rank as good leisure? In reasonably small doses, perhaps so, particularly if the program one is watching challenges the mind or emotions. In truth, if the average person's TV habit consisted of no more than a couple of hours a day, I would not have felt compelled to write this book. Research suggests that, in moderation, watching television does no particular harm—at least not to adults. There's nothing "wrong" with sitting down to watch a favorite sitcom or drama, or a football game, or a news broadcast, or whatever. As we will learn, however, watching television—especially watching a *lot* of television—actually drains our energy. Zoning out in front of the TV is, no doubt, one way to unwind, but, partly for physiological reasons, we seldom come away from hours of television feeling happy and invigorated.

It will come as no surprise that TV viewing is America's number one recreational pursuit. According to recent data from Nielsen Media Research, Americans presently spend an average of 4 hours and 35 minutes each day watching television. (And that doesn't take into account the time some of us spend with computers, playing games or visiting chat rooms.) Moreover, year in and year out, our TV viewing continues to rise. In the year 2000, the television set was on for 7 hours and 40 minutes a day in the typical American home. By 2006, the figure had increased to 8 hours and 14 minutes—roughly a 7.4 percent increase in six years.[1] We are, in short, addicted to television. And the same is true for our children.

Much has been written about how Americans are desperately seeking unity, community, harmony, and purpose. We suffer record levels of obesity, sky-rocketing stress, legions of "lost" youth, and crumbling social networks. People feel rushed, frazzled, dissatisfied, and most of them are in debt. Families are detached, neighbors are strangers, and the "villages" in which our children should be raised have largely ceased to exist. All too commonly, our children spend more hours with some form of electronic entertainment than they do in school. Although what they really crave is our time and attention, we tend instead to surround them with more and more "things" and hope for the best. Many people suspect that television somehow has a role in all this, but they seem to feel powerless, as if they lacked the knowledge or the leverage needed to take control of the situation. That the set might simply be turned off (or even thrown out) does not normally occur as an option.

As a recreation coordinator in Iowa and Oregon, a youth leadership director in Australia and New Zealand, a lecturer at Graceland University and Indiana University, and, for the past two decades, a professor of recreation management at Eastern Washington University, I am naturally curious about how people use their leisure time. I have conducted numerous studies of recreation behavior and have taught hundreds of students about the enjoyment and sense of personal fulfillment that can result from the wise use of leisure. This experience, coupled with my research into what TV-free families do with their free time, has made it apparent that Americans are badly in need of a recreational wake-up call. It is not my intention to berate TV addicts or even to enumerate the harmful consequences of too much television. Plenty of books and articles, some from as early as 1955, have thoroughly tilled that ground. Rather, this book is intended as a reminder that every hour we spend watching television is an hour in which we are *not* doing something else.

Recreation *did* exist before there was television, and it can exist without it. As a matter of fact, for hundreds of TV-free Americans across the country, life without television has proved to be absolutely terrific.

These TV-free individuals belong, of course, to a tiny minority of the population. Some 99 percent of American households have at least one television. In fact, 50 percent of American families own three or more sets.[2] At the same time, even fifteen years ago, nearly half of us felt we were watching too much TV. Moreover, three out of four parents surveyed in a 1994 report from the U.S. Department of Education said they wished that they could limit their children's viewing.[3] It was this last statistical revelation, especially, that intrigued me. If indeed parents were concerned about their children's TV habit—or, for that matter, their own—then why weren't they taking action? What was stopping them? And what did these parents think would be gained if their children watched less television? This led me to wonder about the remaining 1 percent of the population. Thousands of research studies had already documented the detrimental effects of too much television. But what were the inherent benefits (if any)—or, as could be, the inherent disadvantages—of watching little or no television?

This study is the first to provide concrete data on life *without* television. It is based on a survey of hundreds of families who have chosen to live "outside the box." Even though the majority of these people had been TV free for upwards of ten years, many of them reported that they had rarely spoken about what they assumed was their unusual lifestyle. This book aims to shed light on their experience and explore their discoveries—to bring TV-free families out of the closet and into the limelight.

The TV-Free Survey   In November 1999, I placed a small ad in three national magazines requesting that TV-free families and individuals contact me. I was stunned when over five hundred responses poured in. In addition, I received dozens of queries from TV viewers who wanted to know more about life without television—people who had considered getting rid of their set (or sets) but thought the idea too radical. The TV-free individuals who replied to my ad were sent a survey consisting of one hundred questions designed to generate a comprehensive picture of their lives. (The questionnaire is reproduced in Appendix A.) There were questions about basic demographics, consumption patterns, level of education, patterns of social interaction and community involvement, family composition and activities, religious affiliations, computer use, health issues, and recreational preferences. Respondents were also asked to describe their dreams and their regrets and to comment on their overall satisfaction with life.

The 72.7 percent response rate for this lengthy questionnaire—an exceptional rate of response for even a very short survey—represented roughly twelve hundred TV-free men, women, and children. Some of my TV-watching friends laughed and suggested that my respondents must have nothing better to do than to fill out survey questionnaires. The truth was, however, that most of these TV-free individuals had never been asked to talk about their experience and were therefore eager to participate in the research. Even though many of them felt very much alone in their decision to live without television, they did not hesitate to expound on the benefits of the choice they had made. Quite apart from their answers to the survey questions, they supplied me with some four hundred pages of anecdotal information about their reasons for turning off the set and the ways their lives had changed as a result. They also offered insights and advice for others who might wish to cut back on their TV habit or even to eliminate television altogether. Their stories and observations reveal a remarkably passionate commitment to the TV-free life and make a powerful argument not only for its salutary effects but for its many and varied pleasures as well.

My research findings, as well as the general demographics of TV-free families, first appeared in an article published in *Time* magazine.[4] News that many people had made the choice to live outside the box evidently caught the media by surprise. *Family Circle*, *Family Life*, *Good Housekeeping*, *Parenting*, *Parents*, *Reader's Digest*, and *Woman's Day* ran reports of the survey, as did numerous newspapers and radio stations scattered across the country. When Katie Couric of NBC's *Today Show* called to arrange an interview about TV-free families in America, I armed myself with citations and statistics, ready to defend my research against naysayers. In the end, though, every single interviewer with whom I spoke expressed what appeared to be a sincere interest in the TV-free lifestyle. Moreover, many of them at least claimed that they themselves watched very little television or none at all. Even Katie Couric spoke only partially in jest when she mentioned wanting to take her girls off television (although, as she later commented, "It probably wouldn't be a good career move!").

Reality Check   You are not going to live forever, and neither am I. We have only so many hours allotted to us. Much of that time we necessarily devote to earning a living, to household chores and errands, and to eating and sleeping. Over the demands of daily survival we have little choice. But when it comes to our free time, we *do* have options. We can use our leisure time in whatever way we please. I have written this book in hopes of encouraging us to consider the many other things that could be happening during the hours we currently spend in front of the TV and to wonder whether our lives might be more rewarding without television.

The book begins with a brief overview of some of the leisure pursuits we have sacrificed to television over the years and suggests how it is that cultural attitudes toward leisure have contributed to the choice of television as our preferred form of recreation. In the following chapters, we will listen to what TV-free adults and children have to say about their experience and their priorities—what prompted them to banish television from their lives, how they fill up those "empty" hours, and what they feel they have gained as a result. In addition, we will look at the role of television in the lives of our children and discover what happens when children are challenged to go without TV for a period of time. Finally, we will investigate why it is our collective addiction to television holds us so firmly and learn what others have done to overcome it. Children and adults who live very comfortably TV free will tell us what to expect when withdrawing from television and will respond to a series of questions that those who are contemplating such a decision often ask.

In the end, I hope you will be persuaded to experiment—to take a holiday from television and explore other leisure-time pursuits. You might just find that life *outside* the box is far more fascinating and fulfilling.

1: the rise
(and fall)
of recreation

> The human spirit has bounced back
> from worse things than TV.
> —**Mary Pipher,**
> *The Shelter of Each Other*

Archaeologists are uncertain exactly when civilization may be said to have begun, but something resembling it appears to have existed by 6000 BC. Throughout the eight thousand years since, humankind has worked, played, invented, made love, fought, painted, written, read, gardened, raised children, sewed, sawed, solved problems, and resolved difficulties. We still do those things, although in somewhat altered proportions. In addition, we do one thing now that was not possible throughout most of history: instead of actually *doing* these things we push a button and sit in our homes watching actors pretend to do them. This is, in fact, our principal leisure-time activity—so much so that some of us have a hard time imagining life without television. So what exactly did we do before we could simply turn on the TV?

A Brief Look Back Suppose we go back a hundred years, to the start of the twentieth century. What were our favorite recreational pursuits, and what were the values inherent in those pursuits?

Needless to say, children had toys, including one named for Teddy Roosevelt, the great outdoorsman, who loved to hunt bears. Legend has it that on one occasion Roosevelt had a bear cub in his rifle's sights, only to find that he couldn't bring himself to shoot the poor creature. And so, in the opening decade of the century, "Teddy" bears were born. Not long after came Shoenhut's Humpty Dumpty Circus, one of the very first play sets, as well as Crayola crayons and Lionel trains. By 1910, companies like Tootsie Toy and Strombecher were producing miniature cast-iron and tin versions of the Model T and the steam tractor. In addition, young boys made their own toy soldiers by melting lead and pouring it into molds—an admirably creative pursuit, aside from the lead. The early decades of the century also saw the appearance of Erector sets (said to be the first product marketed through a nationwide advertising campaign), Tinker-toys, and Lincoln Logs, as well as a number of children's classics—J. M. Barrie's *Peter Pan*, Kenneth Grahame's *The Wind in the Willows*, Frank Baum's *The Wonderful Wizard of Oz*, Joseph Conrad's *Lord Jim*, and Frances Burnett's *The Secret Garden*.

In 1885, the Boston Sand Gardens—generally held to be the earliest supervised children's recreation program in the United States—opened at the Children's Mission in the city's North End. The idea of a play area filled with piles of sand was borrowed by Dr. Marie E. Zakrzewska from the public park system in Berlin, and by 1900 ten such playgrounds existed in Boston. The year 1906 marked the founding of the Playground Association of America, and soon children all over the country were discovering the joys not only of the sandbox but of the jungle gym, the teeter-totter, and other playground attractions newly installed in public parks. By 1910, supervised recreation programs had sprung up in 336 American cities, and colleges and universities had begun to offer training in recreation design and management. The YMCA and YWCA were already well established when the century opened, but many other youth serving organizations came into existence in its first decades, thanks in part to an American businessman, William Boyce.

The story (possibly apocryphal) goes that while abroad in England, Boyce became disoriented one night in the thick London fog. He despaired of ever finding his way back to his lodgings until a British Boy Scout materialized out of nowhere, helped him get his bearings, and then refused Boyce's offer of a tip in exchange for his good deed. Boyce was so impressed, and so grateful, that he arranged a meeting with Lord Robert Baden-Powell, the founder of the Boy Scout movement in England. Four months later, in February 1910, Boyce founded the Boy Scouts of America. The following year, another American, Juliette Gordon Low, also made the acquaintance of Robert Baden-Powell. At her brother's urging, Robert's sister, Agnes Baden-Powell, had instituted a program designed to instill the values of community service and leadership in girls, and in 1912 Juliette Low organized the first American Girl Guide troops. Within a few years, the Boy Scouts and Girl Scouts (as the movement was renamed in 1913), as well as the Camp Fire Girls, were all active and growing, even in the smallest communities.

On the home front, friends and family gathered together for storytelling sessions and musical evenings, as well as attending church socials, lectures, medicine shows, amateur dramatic productions, puppet shows, and other such entertainments. Penny arcades became popular, as did hoop toys—and, of course, there was baseball. In rural areas, people visited with one another at fairs and on market days. They also held barn raisings, quilting bees, corn-shucking and pie-making contests, and fruit- and vegetable-picking races, all of which afforded ample opportunity for the pleasures of lollygagging. To some extent, recreational activities tended to overlap with chores. But if it ever occurred to our early-twentieth-century forebears that leisure was entirely too much work, there is no record of such an objection.

The years following World War I brought enormous economic growth, along with an eager embrace of all things modern. The universal electrification of cities had made consumer goods, including books and toys, easier to produce. Yo-yos and pogo sticks came into vogue, as did Raggedy Ann and Andy dolls, and bicycles that were affordable and relatively easy to ride appeared on the market. Soda fountains had been in existence for several decades, but during the early 1920s their popularity soared, in part because they offered a replacement for bars, which were forced to close down by the passing of the Prohibition Amendment in 1919. Despite the efforts of the prohibition movement to impose a higher moral standard on the nation, however, the masses proved resistant to sobriety. Some used their spare time to manufacture bathtub gin, while others frequented speakeasies, where they could drink and dance and listen to jazz. The "Roaring Twenties" also marked the dawn of motion pictures, which ushered in the era of mass-market entertainment. Young and old, rich and poor, male and female, people began going out to the cinema.

In addition to the movies, together with the expanding array of toys, books, and sports equipment, the 1920s witnessed one other truly new development in the area of leisure: radio. Only one radio station existed at the start of the decade; by 1930, six hundred programs were being broadcast, and some 40 percent of American households had acquired a radio.[1] Quite apart from its own attractions, listening to the radio had the advantage of not precluding other forms of activity, such as housework, playing cards or doing jigsaws, painting, sewing, working on scrapbooks, and so on. At least in this respect, then, the effect of the radio on home life was to provide an adjunct to, rather than a replacement for, the hearth. Nor did listening to radio encourage mental passivity. Drama programs demanded imaginative and emotional engagement on the part of their audience, and comedy shows often turned on the capacity of listeners to visualize what was going on. Granted, the introduction of radio was not altogether friendly to the old household order. The piano, as a site for social gatherings and entertainment, was pushed to the side, for the most part to reappear only on holidays and other occasions when group singing seemed called for.

The mass unemployment of the Depression years meant that people had very little money for travel and for relatively upscale entertainments such as theatre, opera, or the ballet. Instead, inexpensive pastimes had to be found—playing mumblety-peg, jacks, or marbles, acting out stories, doing crosswords, playing canasta, Monopoly, or Scrabble, and so on. Reading still occupied a place of honor at bedtime, and rapt audiences gathered around the radio for popular shows such as *Flash Gordon*, *Fibber McGee and Molly*, *One Man's Family*, or *Jack Armstrong, the All-American Boy*, all of which premiered in the 1930s. At the same time, the emergency work programs that formed part of Roosevelt's New Deal provided for the construction of parks, resorts, playgrounds, meeting halls, and local concert venues. Between 1933 and 1940, federal work projects were responsible for the creation of some 12,700 playgrounds, 8,500 gymnasiums, 750 swimming pools, 1,000 skating rinks, and over 60 ski jumps.[2]

Motion pictures came on the scene in a major way during the 1920s, especially after the arrival of the "talkies" in 1926, and became, during the

living outside the box

Great Depression, one of the county's most reliable avenues of escape from privation and pervasive financial anxiety. By 1930, roughly four out of five Americans went to the movies at least once a week—some 100 million people out of a population of 123 million.[3] The movies were entertaining, readily available, and cheap to attend. As a form of recreation, they had only one drawback, namely, that viewers were held captive in their seats. Other than necking, there was not much a movie goer could do but sit and watch. Of course, the same could be said of live performances such as theatre, concerts, or puppet shows—although the immediacy of live entertainment to some extent invited audience participation, if only in the form of applause. It was the movies, however, that accustomed people to the idea of sitting in front of a two-dimensional screen as a leisure activity. Arguably, then, the movies paved the way, psychologically, for the role that television would come to play in the lives of American families later in the century.

Then came the Second World War. The day after Pearl Harbor was attacked, roughly 15 million Americans enlisted in the armed services, and the social landscape was utterly transformed. While the United Services Organization (USO) and the Red Cross worked to bring entertainment and other opportunities for recreation to those in the military, dozens of other organizations, many of them newly established, arranged social events, sports programs, and other diversions in an effort to help those at home cope with loneliness and anxiety, as well as sponsoring soldiers' aid bazaars. Of necessity, women entered the workforce, interacting with each other, their families, and the economy in entirely new ways. Teenagers were often forced to grow up rather quickly, as they were needed to look after their younger brothers and sisters while their mothers worked or to take part-time jobs themselves to help support the family. It was, undeniably, a time of hardship and worry. In such circumstances, however, human beings naturally tend to turn to one another for support. If the burden of the war years brought people together as a nation, it also united them in families and local communities.

In short, our twentieth-century forebears did not lack for ways in which to fill up their free time. While it is difficult to generalize about something as multifaceted as leisure, one cannot fail to be struck by the relative preponderance of social or community-oriented activities during the earlier decades of the century. Recreational pursuits tended to be interactive, rather than private, and were more apt to be active than passive.

Enter Television

The end of war inaugurated what would prove to be an unprecedented period of economic growth and prosperity. More women than ever before entered colleges and universities, and the period saw the expansion of professional childcare, along with an explosion in population in the form of the baby boom. Perhaps not surprisingly, the new generation was responsible for many of the fifties' most memorable innovations in the area of leisure. Rock 'n' roll and sock hops hit the scene, and teenagers amassed huge collections of 45s. Now that manufacturing was no longer dominated by the need for military vehicles and equipment, goods of all sorts began to flood the market. In particular, owning a car was now within the economic reach of most families. Urban dwellers headed for the fresh air and open spaces of the suburbs, where they could enjoy a drive-in movie, followed by a burger and shake delivered by one of the roller-skating waitresses at the local drive-in restaurant.

But above all came television. The first fully electronic TV sets had existed as early as 1935, and improvements had continued steadily to be made over the next half-dozen years, until the development of television was temporarily stalled by the war. During the late 1940s, though, television became the rage, and sales began to skyrocket. In 1950, some 9 percent of American households had a television. In the space of only four years, the percentage more than quadrupled, to 55 percent, and by 1960 nine out of ten homes had a TV set. American families were, moreover, glued to their TVs. In the average household in 1960, the television set was on for about five hours a day.[4]

Following shortly on the heels of television came critics of television. *Mass Culture: The Popular Arts in America*, a collection of essays edited by Bernard Rosenberg and David Manning White, appeared in 1957 and was destined to become a classic. In the arena of entertainment, television was held to exemplify Gresham's Law, namely, that bad money drives good money out of circulation. Similarly, the argument ran, bad enter-

living outside the box

tainment, because it is cheaper to produce and easier to understand and absorb, will tend to drive out the good.[5] Mass culture, in other words, works to undermine high culture.

Among the early critics of television was Jay B. Nash, whose *Philosophy of Recreation and Leisure* was first published in 1953. Over fifty years ago, Nash was already complaining that TV ate up most of our time. He worried that, as a nation, we were becoming content to watch rather than act, and he was concerned about the declining role of conversation, reading, and play in American life—that is, about the deteriorating quality of our leisure time. In fact, Nash developed a model for assessing the depth of an individual's engagement with life. Shaped like a triangle, his model described four levels.[6] At the peak of the triangle was Level Four, which Nash labeled "creative participation." Those who participate creatively include the inventor, the artist, the "idea" person. Level Three, a quarter of the way down, was designated "active participation." At this level we would find the actor, the musician, the mountain climber, the volunteer, the athlete, the builder. Another quarter of the way down was Level Two, that of "emotional participation," the home of the reader, the avid fan, the good listener. Each of these three levels of engagement provides enrichment to the participant, possibly even life-changing enrichment.

At the base of the triangle, at Level One, Nash placed "passive participation," or what he termed "spectatoritis": mindless amusements, escape from monotony, killing time, and other simple antidotes to boredom—the "mental flophouses."[7] And, alas, Level One is where Americans spend most of their spare time. There are no active, creative, or deeply memorable experiences at Level One. There are pulp novels, the tabloids, and other such sensationalist fare, as well as acres of AM radio, but the chief tenant of Nash's ground floor is television. Granted, some television programs bring their audience to a state of active emotional engagement and so could qualify for Level Two—and if one were watching a program in which one is deeply engaged while at the same time riding an exercycle, perhaps such an experience would qualify for Level Two-Point-Five or something. But the majority of TV programming today offers only one thing: escape.

Below Level One were yet two more levels, Zero and Sub-Zero, the provinces of abuse, addiction, mischief making, and crime. Whatever one may say about television, it presumably scores over mainlining heroin or robbing gas stations. Still, Level One is not much to shoot for. Indeed, by Nash's criteria, the average American's use of leisure time was, and still is, far from impressive.

No doubt these early critics of TV were guilty of a certain elitism, inasmuch as part of their complaint had to do with artistic standards (an area in which television has traditionally earned low marks) and with the decline of more "refined" pursuits. All the same, their concern with the quality of our leisure—with the dwindling popularity of recreational pursuits that involved the exercise of imagination and creativity or in some way broadened the mind—was sincere. Perhaps more to the point, it would prove to be well founded.

Every new artifact of culture, be it a product or an idea, modifies the way we think and behave and therefore harbors the potential for negative consequences. These consequences may not be initially apparent to us, however, emerging only after the innovation has settled into our lives. As a communications medium, television has been a marvelous advance, capable of delivering information more efficiently and in many ways more effectively than ever before. Precisely because it is a visual medium, television has brought the world into our homes with an immediacy that radio could never achieve. The question has to do with who's in charge. "There has never been a single TV set that caused brain damage or committed a crime," writes Jim Trelease in his *Read-Aloud Handbook*. "People control it and use it; it is the *overviewing* of television that causes the problem."[8] That, and the fact that we have allowed television programming to be dictated by commercial interests, with the result that the phenomenal potential of television has largely been trivialized. All the same, just because the mental flophouse exists doesn't mean we have to live in it. The decision is ours.

living outside the box

2: fear of leisure

Nothing—not low education, not full-time work, not long commutes in urban agglomerations, not poverty or financial distress—is more broadly associated with civic disengagement and social disconnection than is dependence on television for entertainment.

—Robert Putnam,
Bowling Alone: The Collapse and Revival of American Community

Like people everywhere, Americans long for genuine leisure—time when we can choose what to do, rather than being forced by authority, circumstance, or tradition. Ask anyone, or ask yourself: What are your dreams and desires? Perhaps you've always wanted to learn Swedish, to grow your own vegetables, to read all of *The Remembrance of Things Past*, to start an exercise program, to climb Mt. McKinley, to learn to quilt, or to play Mozart on the piano. Has a novel been simmering in you for years, waiting for the moment when you will have enough time to commit yourself to writing it? Have you always hoped to find yourself free simply to lie on a beach, or even just in a hammock somewhere, owing nothing to anyone? Maybe you dream of building closer family relationships. Or perhaps you would like to travel without feeling the constant pressure to return to work, to "get back in harness."

True, some of these projects would require considerable training, planning, and/or money, as well as large blocks of time. But others would involve only an hour or two here and there, or at most a few hours of regularly scheduled effort. "*Only* an hour or two!" you exclaim. "*At most* a few regularly scheduled hours!" And who could blame you for that response? Our society is haunted, dominated, tyrannized by a pervasive sense of time crunch, the Procrustean clock, the shadow of the hours growing shorter and shorter.

Over the past decades, stress has emerged as an increasingly pervasive psychological ailment and social problem. Thanks to the industrial and technological revolutions, we are surrounded by labor-saving devices, fast food restaurants, and assorted other conveniences that decrease the hours we must spend on basic chores. Moreover, new workweek models have given many working Americans greater flexibility. The forty-hour week is still with us, but innovative approaches to scheduling, including the option of working at home, offer employees greater freedom to arrange their leisure time as suits them best. We also enjoy an unprecedented standard of living, in which what were formerly household luxuries have become commonplace. We are able to choose from a myriad of transportation options and recreational possibilities, including socially and physically enriching opportunities for our children. And yet nearly everyone seems pressed for time, on edge, perennially restless. In 1965, one in four Americans characterized themselves as "always rushed." By 1992, one in three felt that way.[1]

In terms of media equipment, American children are extraordinarily privileged, often growing up in a home with two or three TVs, at least one DVD player, several audio tape decks, a CD player or two, a video-game player, and at least one computer.[2] Yet many among our youth are at risk for underachievement and social disenchantment. Reading scores have been declining steadily since the mid-1960s, and teachers complain of having to "dumb down" required reading lists.[3] In a study conducted in 2003 by the Centers for Disease Control, children's fitness scores were so low that they shocked even the researchers, who viewed the alarming rise in the incidence of obesity and Type II diabetes among children as one critical consequence of an increasingly sedentary lifestyle.[4] Although parents say they would like to limit their children's TV viewing, nearly two-thirds (65 percent) of children aged six or under live in a home where the television is on at least half the time, even when no one is really watching

living outside the box

it, and over a third (36 percent) in households where the TV is on all or most of the time. Moreover, nearly half (45 percent) of all parents say that when they have something important to do, it is quite likely that they will use TV as a babysitter.[5] And TV is only the tip of the iceberg. Video arcades are everywhere and are typically thronged with children. Game Boys emerge from our children's pockets at recess, on lunch hours, and in virtually every other spare minute, while iPods and MP3s invite them to retreat behind a wall of sound. A report released by the Kaiser Family Foundation in March 2005 revealed that children between the ages of eight and eighteen spent an average of 8 hours and 33 minutes each day engaging with media of some sort.[6]

The one sure thing we gain each year is stuff—stuff to fill our homes, garages, and storage spaces. The one thing we seem to lose each year is time—time for a long leisurely evening of doing nothing in particular, or for a bike ride or walk, or for talking with friends or family, or for being alone with our thoughts. How has this happened? Part of the problem is that much of the leisure time made available by technological advances, job sharing, efficient transport, home-office trends, and the like has been gobbled up by television. For over fifty years now, our TV habit has slowly been eroding the free time that technology was supposed to render more abundant. We've been drawn gradually, though not altogether innocently, into the belief that the screen is the new hearth of the home.

Robert Putnam, a professor of economics at Harvard University and the author of *Bowling Alone: The Collapse and Revival of American Community*, studies "social capital," the connections and relationships that develop between individuals as they build community in social groups— through membership in service clubs, churches, civic leagues, or political parties, for example, or by participating in neighborhood projects or local PTAs. Drawing on twenty-five years' worth of data from the Roper Social and Political Trends and the DDB Needham Lifestyle surveys, Putnam discovered that, on average, couples spent three to four times as many minutes watching TV as they did talking to each other and six to seven times as many as they devoted to community activities outside the home.[7] Interviewed on National Public Radio about his findings, Putnam commented: "Electronic entertainment, especially television, has profoundly privatized leisure time. Time [spent] watching television is a direct drain upon involvement in social-capital building activities. It may contribute to up to 40 percent of the decline in involvement with groups over the past twenty-five years." As he went on to remark, "Americans watch *Friends*—they don't *have* friends anymore."[8]

Why is this? How has television come to masquerade as a family member in millions of American homes? In a sense, the answer is obvious. We watch TV because television is readily available, affordable, and intimately positioned. The TV set has become a standard piece of furniture in our "living" rooms, our "family" rooms, even in our bedrooms and bathrooms. It is our default option. Apart from working, the only thing we do more than watch TV is sleep. Engaging with it does not require that we dress up, drive, spend a lot of money, or exercise our minds and bodies. All television asks of us is that we press a button, sit back, and zone out. Or doze off. The January 1996 Harper's Index reported that one in four Americans falls asleep at least three nights each week in front of the television. Moreover, even though there may be more than one person in the room, watching television is a fundamentally solitary activity. Community involvement and volunteerism have continued to drop among adults as our TV viewing has increased over the years. We have indeed become a nation of spectators.

The four and a half hours a day that the average American spends more or less immobile in front of the television set add up to 1,673 hours each year. By the time we reach the age of sixty-five, these daily devotions will have occupied us for more than twelve years—enough time to complete the requirements for a bachelor's degree, a master's, and a Ph.D. Twelve years is the approximate length of our retirement, and greater than the entire span of our adolescence. But those years are gone. And what do we have to show for them? What have we given our children? What does our behavior teach them? Quite simply, that it is better to be passive than active, better to live vicariously than actually, better to be silent than to converse.

A Nation of Puritans Some of the great Greek philosophers extolled the virtues of leisure as necessary to what we would call the good life. Plato felt that music and gymnastics, when engaged in regularly, provided both physical and spiritual rejuvenation. Socrates argued that leisure was best spent in the pursuit of knowledge, which would in turn allow us to choose the greatest pleasures. In "Leisure and Civility: Reflections on a Greek Ideal," John Hemingway writes that, in Aristotle's view, life should be devoted not only to noble and divine thought but to deeds civic, productive, and refreshing.[9] In fact, the early Greeks were among the first to ponder the importance of play—to acknowledge our need to allow both the mind and the body time for relaxation. Their heritage is with us still, not only in their ideas but in the toys they invented, such as jacks, tops, and marbles, and, of course, in the Olympic Games.

And yet in America this aspect of the Greek heritage has not had an easy time of it. From the earliest colonial times, well before the adage "An idle brain is the Devil's playground" made its way into in H. G. Bohn's *Hand-Book of Proverbs* (1855), the Puritan ethic held sway, and with it came a deeply ingrained suspicion of "free time." Leisure was associated with sloth, one of the seven deadly sins, and with the failure to demonstrate the robust state of one's soul by means of productivity and the wealth that resulted, whereby God's blessing was made manifest. Scholarly pursuits were countenanced only in ecclesiastical contexts. It was all right for Jonathan Edwards, Cotton Mather, and Edward Taylor to devote themselves to study, for they were men of God, and their intellectual labors were carried out on the community's behalf. They were guided by the Almighty in their pursuits, whereas, left to our own devices, we ordinary folk were prone to the temptations of Satan.

No doubt this attitude retarded the development of a leisure ethic such as the Greeks espoused. Moreover, as Jay Nash argued fifty years ago, "In America there has been no leisure-time philosophy for the simple reason that up to this generation there has been no leisure."[10] Nash may have been overstating his position, but his point is well taken. Startling though it may be, in some parts of the country our society is barely four generations removed from frontier realities that demanded clearing the land for farming, constructing our own dwellings, sewing our own clothing, and attending to countless daily chores—all the while maintaining readiness to fend off violent attack from marauders and hostile natives. This is obviously not to say that our ancestors had no free time or that purely recreational pursuits did not exist. But only comparatively recently have working Americans been in a position to set aside time specifically for relaxation and has "leisure" thus emerged as an independent concept, a distinct category of our lives.

Historically, then, one can understand why Americans might have difficulty embracing leisure. Not only do memories of the frontier still linger in our collective psyche, but our cultural heritage has taught us to regard recreational pursuits as somewhat suspect. Perhaps, too, free time makes us nervous simply because no one is there to tell us what to do. As Mihaly Csikszentmihalyi notes in *Finding Flow: The Psychology of Engagement with Everyday Life*, Americans seem vulnerable to what the early-twentieth-century psychoanalyst Sándor Ferenczi called the "Sunday neurosis," a term that referred to the bouts of hysteria and depression that his patients frequently experienced on Sundays, when they were without the direction provided by work. In Csikszentmihalyi's view, "The average person is ill equipped to be idle." He cites the 1958 annual report of the Group for the Advancement of Psychiatry—written when conveniences were beginning to free up greater amounts of time and satisfaction with life appeared to be on the upswing: "For many Americans," the report concluded, "leisure is dangerous."[11] Indeed, more symptoms of illness, more crimes, more suicides, and more voluntary disappearances are reported on holidays, vacations, and weekends than on regular workdays.

Not altogether surprisingly, Americans observe fewer holidays than any other developed nation. Ours is, moreover, the only country in which a reasonable amount of vacation time is given as a reward for seniority rather than as a basic job benefit.[12] As Joe Robinson, one of the contributors to *Take Back Your Time: Fighting Overwork and Time Poverty in America*, informs us: "While our colleagues in Paris and Melbourne get four to five weeks of paid leave by law each year—six or more by collective agreement—Americans are stuck with 8.1 days after the first year on the job, and 10.2 days after three years—by far the shortest vacations in the

living outside the box

industrialized world." The United States has the distinction of being the only developed nation that has yet to require by law a minimum amount of paid leave. "It's not that U.S. companies can't implement real vacations," Robinson points out. "They just don't want to."[13]

In short, the Protestant ethic, with its stress on the virtues of work and struggle, is not only alive but thriving. As an attitude toward life, it most often, and most clearly, finds expression in terms of goals and accomplishments. Americans tend to be at their most focused and energetic when working to achieve specific ends and at their most relaxed and self-assured when reflecting on ends achieved, that is, on their successes. In the absence of a set goal, however—when we are at long last face to face with the prospect of genuine leisure time—we don't seem to know what to do with ourselves. In our uncertainty, we are prone to engage in somewhat frenetic forms of recreation, especially if these afford us opportunities for conspicuous consumption and status display. As Juliet Schor argues in *The Overworked American*, "The ability to use leisure is not a natural talent, but one that must be cultivated. If we veer too much toward work, our leisure skills will atrophy."[14] As soon as the immediate pressure to achieve is lifted, we very often find ourselves seized with an anxious sense of aimlessness, of being at "loose ends," that is perfectly answered by the hypnotic power of television. It is as though once we've done our work, once we've made our daily contribution, we are drained of initiative, and so we feel we *deserve* to sit still, whether alone or together, and passively gaze at a screen.

Here we encounter one of the more insidious effects of our workaholic tendencies: exhaustion. The length of our workweek, coupled with the brevity of our vacations, only serves to fuel the appeal of television. As John de Graaf, originator of the "Take Back Your Time Day" initiative and a producer at KCTS television in Seattle, commented:

> Statistics show that the more a country's people work in a year, the more they watch television. The United States, with the longest working hours, watches the most TV, while Norway, with the shortest, watches the least. The correlation is very clear. The reason is that TV is an activity that appeals to

people who are exhausted and drained and want to be entertained. People with fewer work hours have the energy to meet friends, read, and do other things. . . . If we can get our act together in the U.S. to decrease the number of work hours comparable to other developed nations, the free time will lead to less TV viewing and open up more possibilities for "good" leisure.[15]

To be fair, a few recent developments suggest that some of us may have reached our limit. For example, quilting groups are forming once again. Rarely do members gather around a large wooden frame, as they once did, with as many as twenty people working together on a single quilt. But they do meet around their common interest in the activity, and the chatter of conversation, over the hum of sewing machines, is no doubt much as before. In 2000, concerned that our fund of social capital was running dangerously low, participants in Harvard University's Saguaro Seminar on Civic Engagement in America issued a report, titled *Better Together*, that outlined a program of sustained social change designed to reverse the trend toward civic apathy. As Robert Putnam, author of *Bowling Alone* and the founder of the seminar, points out, "We now see a public that is withdrawing from communal life, choosing to live alone and play alone." But a "civic renaissance" is possible, he argues, and "the future well-being of our nation depends on it."[16]

The simplicity movement, which seeks to foster more balanced, healthy, and sustainable lives, is also gaining recognition and acceptance. The basic premise of the movement is that, for the sake of ourselves and our planet, we must learn to "downshift." We need to work less and consume less—not in the service of some sort of ascetic ideal but in order to regain a measure of sanity. Organizations such as the Center for the New American Dream, Work to Live, Free Our Time, and the Small Planet Fund promote "conscious living." The movement, which is now worldwide, launched the first ever "Take Back Your Time Day" on October 24, 2003, in an effort to focus attention on the incredible busyness of our lives, and legislation that would increase vacation time is in the works.

living outside the box

Privileged and Impoverished   We *are* very busy, although we are also very privileged. But if our lives are busy, so, one could argue, were those of our early-twentieth-century counterparts—who, after all, had to do without prepackaged foods, microwave ovens, side-by-side refrigerators, garbage disposals, washers and dryers, shopping malls, and so forth. As we have seen, they sometimes had little choice but to combine work and play. So what is the difference? Why do we feel so pressed for time, and why has stress so overwhelmed our lives?

Perhaps, for one thing, in our desire not to miss out, we have allowed technology to make us too accessible. At home, we are plagued by calls from telephone solicitors; we can't keep up with our email (even if much of it is spam); our cell phones ring while we're driving or shopping for groceries or taking a bath—and we answer them. Seldom do we sit still, in silence. For those on the go, Chevrolet now offers the Warner Brothers Edition of the Venture van, which comes equipped with an overhead fold-down color monitor, DVD player, CD player, video game and camcorder inputs, four sets of wireless headphones, and a wireless remote. Seldom do we sit still, in silence.

We are also working too hard—not at chores but at our jobs, jobs that we may or may not enjoy but that we hope will earn us the money we need to afford all the things we feel we must have. At the same time, as both research studies and common sense suggest, children, teens, and all the rest of us seem to be searching for something money cannot buy. As our look back at the initial decades of the twentieth century revealed, leisure pursuits once served to bring people together more often than to isolate them. Perhaps, then, between rushing around and collapsing in front of the TV, we have forgotten how to be with each other. Perhaps we are not busy so much as lonely.

3: a word from our sponsors

For me, if there was any one reason to get rid of TV, it was commercials. I'm fine with capitalism and the free market, but my mind isn't free. Nor are my kid's minds. They're going to have to work much harder now to sell us products and ideas.

—TV-free father
from Edina, Minnesota

I remember seeing an advertisement for a car dealership some years ago that caught my attention. "Why just keep up with the Joneses," the ad asked, "if you can kick their butts?" As Thorsten Veblen famously argued over a century ago in *The Theory of the Leisure Class* (1899), Americans seem driven to impress by means of acquisition. We are besieged by commercial messages that exhort us to reject last year's car, computer, toy, or fashion trend, and we comply. Owning the newest and shiniest somehow lends us a feeling of security, even of power. But why do we give in to these fundamentally artificial needs? Are we, as a nation, in the grips of some sort of collective inferiority complex? Why have we allowed the commercial world to tell us how to act and what to buy, wear, eat, and drink?

Brain Rinsing

Doubtless a single advertisement does little psychological damage, but eight messages can make a point stick, to say nothing of eighty. On upwards of five hundred TV channels some 1,200 ads are broadcast daily—as many as eighty in the space of an hour.[1] Spend an hour watching daytime television, and you will spend about seventeen minutes watching commercials. And each commercial, however brief, and whether entertaining or dull, diminishes the time available for actual programming, which is presumably what people want to see. Even the once-sacred television news has fallen victim: roughly one-quarter of a typical network news broadcast is now devoted to commercials.[2] Not only is the number of ads on the rise each year, but, as most viewers will have noticed, the same ads are aired repeatedly in the course of a program. Nor have producers remained content to bunch commercials at the beginning or end of shows. Instead, they interrupt programs, with increasing frequency, to reinforce again and again the will of their sponsors—that people be induced to buy.

TV ads have also grown shorter over the years, now often running only ten seconds instead of thirty, which of course allows more ads to be crammed into a single commercial break. Whereas older-style commercials tended to focus on a vignette—a brief story that delivered a message, which the makers of the product hoped would prove persuasive—today's ads are oriented more toward grabbing and holding the viewer's attention. The assumption (apparently correct) is that the next time consumers are shopping, the mere recollection of the product's name will be enough to spur a purchase. Rather than information about the presumed virtues of a product, what counts is brand-name recognition. Never in history have we been so surrounded by logos, labels, and slogans. And it's not only the commercials themselves: it's product placement. Marketers have discovered that people pay attention to what characters in TV shows wear, what they eat and drink, what kind of car they drive, and what they have in their homes and offices. Those who manufacture such products are more than willing to make their wares available for use as props or set decoration. Let a brand-name item appear on the screen, and sales are sure to follow. Product placement has likewise invaded the movies—which viewers increasingly watch in the privacy of their homes, on their TVs.

It is not news that the lifestyles depicted in many commercials are well beyond the average American's reach—but this is the point of the exercise. The moguls of commerce work tirelessly to define our every need,

living outside the box

desire, and fantasy. Some blame the hundreds of commercials that many of us view each day for the narcissism, the sense of entitlement, and the dissatisfaction—even rage—now rampant in our society. In the opinion of sociologist Eugene Halton, consumer culture boils down to a form of psychological enslavement, in which the promise of happiness is used as the bait. Viewers are "brain rinsed," he argues, into believing that all forms of satisfaction are available for purchase: "If you buy this car, you can have a relationship with a beautiful woman like the one on the commercial. If you buy this brand of clothing, people will be impressed with you."[3]

Television is, in short, consumed with consumerism. The cumulative effect of this parade of consumer items is profound. "Every time I turn on the TV, I'm reminded of what I don't have," writes John Monczunski, an associate editor at *Notre Dame Magazine*. "Sure, sooner or later most of this stuff will end up in the Prairie View landfill south of town. And we both know I'll just want more. As Miss Piggy would say, more is more." His point about our throwaway culture is worth underscoring. Americans, who constitute about 6 percent of the world's population, consume over a third of the planet's resources. We also produce a vastly disproportionate share of the inorganic wastes that wind up as landfill around the world. Moreover, as Monczunski goes on to point out, thanks to the globalization of communications media, "consumer culture is taking root in the most foreign soil. Now everyone in sight of a TV wants the same stuff."[4] But this is simply not possible. The planet is already in ecological overdrive. "To supply all 6 billion plus humans with the resources and land needed to absorb the wastes Americans use and create today," writes Zachary Smith, "we would need three Earths."[5] If people in other countries were to follow our lead, soon there would be nothing left to fill.

Our drive to possess has also turned us into a nation of debtors. According to a January 31, 2006, report on NPR's *Morning Edition,* consumption rates have reached an all-time high, while savings rates have fallen to -0.05 percent, the lowest they have been since the Depression. On average, Americans were saving a little under 4 percent of their income in 1997—half of what Germans were saving at the time, and a quarter of the average for Japan.[6] By the end of 2004 we were down to 0.2 percent, and the rate sometimes dipped below zero. In comparison, in the European Union the average was 12 percent, while people in some third world nations were managing to save nearly a quarter of their wages. For someone earning an annual salary of $40,000, a 0.2 percent savings rate works out to about $1.50 a week. Only twenty-five years ago, Americans were saving nearly 10 percent of their wages. Now we're living paycheck to paycheck.[7]

In the meanwhile, credit card debt tripled over the course of the 1990s. "The average American household carried about $9,000 in credit card debt during the year 2002," report the authors of *Affluenza: The All-Consuming Epidemic*, with fewer than a third of Americans paying off their credit card balances every month in order to avoid interest charges.[8] By 2004, approximately 1.6 million Americans were filing for bankruptcy every year, at an unprecedented rate of one about every fifteen seconds.[9] Although catastrophic medical bills or loss of employment is often the root of the problem, a large proportion of these filings can be traced to reckless spending, which the deregulation of the credit card industry in the early 1980s did wonders to promote. Even wealthy people are in debt. The unrelenting sense that something is lacking—the conviction that unless we have such-and-such we are somehow incomplete—prompts us to buy the item now and worry about how to pay for it later. All this spells not affluence but dissatisfaction.

Multiple reasons exist for the sad state of our finances, but one thing is clear: we are constantly being encouraged to spend beyond our means. We are bombarded by messages that tell us we're not rich enough, or stylish, or attractive, or successful enough, unless we own a particular product.

In an essay entitled "All That Glitters," author Mary Pipher tells of a visit she made to a family from northern Iraq that she had gotten to know in the course of researching a book on immigrants. Zena, the mother, led Pipher into the living room, where her two younger children were watching cartoons. The youngsters were sporting Spiderman T-shirts, and Star Wars and Pokémon plastic figures were strewn among videos and other toys. Pipher also noticed an ashtray and a pack of Marlboros, new since her previous visit. Together, they watched an animated version of *The Wizard of Oz*, evidently a favorite of Zena's oldest child, a daughter, who had a stuffed dog named Toto. When Pipher offered to read to the children, they

living outside the box

gathered around eagerly. It was her daughter's birthday, and Zena had worked all day to prepare a feast—homemade flatbread, roast chicken, and vegetables, which were served along with potato chips and Cokes. The family sat among the toys on the living room floor, passing dishes and eating with their fingers, the television blaring in the background.

The family had come from a rural area where mass-market consumer goods were virtually unheard of. Now they were in the process of assimilating to a new culture and absorbing its values. Thrust headlong into American abundance, they were being taught that everyone *needs* cigarettes, soda pop, snack foods, action-packed video games, cartoon figures, toy weapons, and fancy dolls. As Pipher comments: "Television, their main educator, told them lies—that happiness comes from buying consumer goods and unhealthy foods, that most Americans are rich, and that expensive cars and clothes are important. There were no ads for the joy of quiet time, calmness, walks, gardening, looking at sunsets, visiting with neighbors, or reading to children." Living, at last, in a country theoretically bright with possibility, they sat before an electronic box as it repeated endlessly its formula for a successful and satisfying life.[10]

TV Advertising . . . or Child Abuse?

John de Graaf is very much aware of the ramifications of brain rinsing. In 1997, he and Vivia Boe produced the classic documentary *Affluenza*, a term they defined as "an epidemic of stress, overwork, waste, and indebtedness caused by a dogged pursuit of the American Dream." In one segment of the film, a young child is seen watching a TV commercial promoting something allegedly indispensable (the "you-can't-live-without-it" appeal) and supposedly quite affordable. The ad urges children to get their parents to dial an 800 number and purchase the item ("Run and do it right *now!*"). The film follows the child as he gets up and dashes over to his father, who is working on the computer and shoos him away. Then he tries his mother, who is talking on the phone and says, "Not now, honey." Finally, the boy locates his father's wallet and removes a credit card. When his father catches him in the act of dialing the 800 number himself, we watch as the boy storms off.

"There's always Grandma," he says angrily. "She'll buy it for me." Later in the film, another young boy, whose family lives in low-income housing, asks his mother to buy him a pair of trendy, and very expensive, athletic shoes he has seen in a commercial featuring Michael Jordan. The mother gently explains that the family can't afford them. But, as she rather ruefully tells us later in the film, her son's two aunts felt that he should have the shoes, and so they bought them for him.

During a "Television and Children" workshop I conducted in 2004, one mother recounted what I thought was a rather harrowing story. Her two-year-old child had seen a commercial for one of the latest toys from Burger King, which she desperately wanted. The child begged and complained and whined for hours, throughout the day and into the evening, driving her parents to distraction. They were astonished, the mother said, at the ferocity of this very small child's expressions of need. The next morning, when the whining and complaining went on unabated, she finally caved in, bundled up her toddler, and drove several miles to a Burger King to get the toy. "The poor kids who worked there had to go through three boxes to find the right one," she told us. "And then, when they found it, instead of the $1.00 it used to be, the price had gone up. We paid $2.50 for the breakfast meal and another $1.99 for the stupid toy!"

As she was describing this saga, I crossed my fingers, hoping that she would stick to her guns and refuse to reinforce the message that material possessions are the source of happiness. But in the end her child wore her down. And this was a mother who was really *trying*, who was attending a workshop on parenting skills, who wanted the best for her children. She was very angry at the power of that commercial over her toddler, as well as angry with herself for ultimately capitulating. Imagine the millions of parents who don't care as much, those who have little or no idea what their children are watching on television and casually acquiesce in their everyday demands. Unfortunately, though, the fact remains that our impressionable children are so inundated with clever promotions that even the most resolute parents find it almost impossible to stand up against the barrage of products—that, and their children's persistent nagging. A survey conducted in May 2002 by the Center for a New American Dream discovered that children between the ages of twelve and seventeen will ask for products they have seen advertised an average of nine times in order to convince their parents to make a purchase. Moreover, 55 percent of the children surveyed said that their efforts were usually successful.[11]

In short, harrowing or not, the mother's story is probably all too common. In 1983, marketers spent about $100 million on TV advertising aimed at children; today they spend something on the order of 150 times that amount—$15 billon each year.[12] Evidently, though, their investment pays off. In 2000, children influenced the spending of more than $500 billion by their parents, up from $5 billion annually in the 1960s and $50 billion in the 1980s.[13] Moreover, thanks to popular children's networks and their multimillion-dollar preschool programs, even toddlers now represent potential advertising dollars. There are, for example, some 150 different products linked to *Dora the Explorer*, a show aimed at preschoolers, with a combined price tag of over $3,000, while SpongeBob's grinning face now adorns boxes of macaroni and cheese. As Cyma Karghami, president of Nickelodeon Television, sees it, such merchandising, far from being exploitative, is "really helping kids connect, in some ways emotionally, to the characters they love."[14]

In other words, marketers have figured out that if they can lure children into watching television (that is, commercials) at an early age, they have a good chance of hooking them for life—and the average American child now watches some 40,000 commercials each year.[15] As Douglas Rushkoff, a professor of media studies at New York University and the consulting producer for a *Frontline* documentary called "The Merchants of Cool," put it: "Kids are moving though a reality in which they're being marketed to 24-7. It's almost to the point where it's in their sleep, or certainly on their bedsheets. . . . There is no such thing as enough in our current economic model, and kids are bearing the brunt of that." Rushkoff further observed that because our consumption-driven economy now depends on children to make decisions about what to purchase—about how a family's resources should be spent—it forces our children to behave like adults.[16]

Like greedy adults, one might say. Roy Fox, author of *Harvesting Minds: How TV Commercials Control Kids*, cites research indicating that commercials not only make children more materialistic but also generate friction between them and their parents and discourage the formation of "moral and ethical" values.[17] In the opinion of child psychologist Allen Kanner, the problem is not merely that all this advertising has instilled excessively materialist values in our children—although it has surely done that. But the advertising blitz has also been responsible for what he terms a "narcissistic wounding": it has convinced children that unless they can command an unending supply of new merchandise, they are inferior. "The whole enterprise of advertising," Kanner argues, "is about creating insecure people who believe they need to buy things to be happy."[18] Similarly, sociologist Juliet Schor has linked the assault of consumer culture on our children to low self-esteem, as well as to depression, anxiety, and conflicts with parents.[19]

In one especially alarming development, TV marketers have begun systematically pursuing children in our public schools. In 1989, Christopher Whittle, president of Whittle Communications and former owner of *Esquire* magazine, set up a pilot news program in six school systems that has proved to be immensely successful. Now called Channel One, the program offers a twelve-minute broadcast that purports to deliver news about the world to millions of students in thousands of schools across the country each day. If a school signs up—and the schools that do tend to be located in relatively low-income communities, where both teachers and textbooks are often in short supply—it receives a satellite dish and TV/VCRs for every classroom, for as long as the subscription is maintained. Sounds like a worthy enterprise, right? But there's a catch. Each twelve-minute broadcast actually provides only ten minutes of news— and most of that focuses on sports, weather (including natural disasters), and various lightweight features and profiles. The other two minutes consist of commercials for video games, sneakers, and other such merchandise, as well as a variety of snack foods and candy—items often readily available in the school's vending machines.

As the Center for Commercial-Free Public Education points out, twelve minutes of Channel One daily adds up to six full school days a year spent watching TV, one full day of which is devoted to nothing but commercial messages. A thirty-second commercial spot on Channel One costs roughly $200,000 (about twice as much as a prime-time network ad), but the profits for manufacturers and retailers are commensurate. Any educational profit the children may derive is secondary. In fact, one research study concluded that "Channel One costs taxpayers $1.8 billion annually in lost instructional time, including $300 million in class time lost to commercials."[20] In other words, children are now being "taught" by people whose overriding purpose is to sell something. Incredibly, there now exist textbooks that relate the "story" of Tootsie Rolls or Twinkies, as though their "invention" had historical significance.

Even when the TV programs children see in school are commercial free, the addictive power of the medium is insidious. Hannah, a second-grader in the Spokane public school system, is required to watch an hour of public television each day in her classroom—*Reading Rainbow* and *Between the Lions*, PBS programs that ostensibly promote reading skills and foster a love of books. But Hannah was having trouble learning to read. When her teacher recommended that she stay in during recess to take advantage of reading tutors, Hannah's mother objected, knowing that her very active child badly needed time to run around and play. The teacher's response spoke volumes. "But the only other hour available for tutoring is the TV hour," she explained, "and no one wants to miss out on that."

To make matters worse, a wave of media mergers has narrowed down control over the vast majority of television programming into a handful of corporate conglomerates that seek above all to maximize profits. The web of business relationships extends to politicians who allow themselves to be bribed by these massive corporations into voting to permit them to bypass government regulations on advertising and fair trade (to say nothing of the rules of evidence in news reporting). Writing in *The Other Parent*, James Steyer notes that media moguls such as Rupert Murdoch and Haim Saban have made political contributions totaling millions over the years, throwing their financial support behind politicians who have opposed efforts to strengthen FCC regulations regarding the length, frequency, and content of on-air advertising—regulations that would have protected children, at least to some degree, from runaway merchandising. In addition, Steyer argues, since Murdoch launched Fox Television in the mid-1980s, the network has "pushed the envelope on risqué programming."[21]

Steyer traces the growing popularity of merchandise-driven cartoons the likes of *Power Rangers* or *Big Bad BeetleBorgs*, as well as a host of other low-budget violent action adventures, to a collaboration between Murdoch and Saban that dates back to 1993. In the wake of the deregulation spree of the 1980s, which knocked down the barriers that had previously prevented sponsors of TV programs from functioning as producers, toy companies began to fund children's programs such us *Strawberry Shortcake*, *The Smurfs*, and *Thundercats*.[22] Producers of these cartoons relentlessly plug licensed merchandise to young consumers—who are, alas, especially vulnerable to commercial messages. "While older children and adults understand the inherent bias of advertising," says child psychologist Dale Kunkel, "younger children do not, and therefore tend to interpret commercial claims and appeals as accurate and truthful information."[23] Or, as the American Academy of Pediatrics reminds us, "Many younger children cannot discriminate between what they see and what is real."[24] They have yet to develop the critical skills that will eventually enable them to distinguish fact from fiction. Until they do, they need to be able to trust adults. The stories they are told, however, and the lessons they learn from them, no longer come from families, schoolteachers, churches, or neighbors. They emanate from a medium controlled by people who have small care for the quality of their lives. "We have become a nation that places a lower priority on teaching its children how to thrive socially, intellectually, even spiritually, than it does on training them to consume," writes sociologist Juliet Schor. "The long-term consequences of this development are ominous."[25]

Life Without Commercial Interruptions

A poster designed by *AdBusters* depicts a young boy engrossed in a book while in the background a TV set waves its antennalike arms wildly, trying desperately to get his attention. A 2004 ad for *Sports Illustrated* shows a child laughing and dangling upside down by his knees on a swing set. The caption says, "Billy's dad took his TV away—punishment or prize?" All the same, many parents wonder whether banishing the TV from the household truly is an option.

Not only is the TV-free life possible, however: it is profitable. These profits include hours available for conversation, hobbies, exercise, or forms of entertainment that allow for participation and engagement. They also include the thousands of dollars *not* spent on the products that TV advertising so incessantly flogs. When the TV-free parents who responded to my survey were asked how often their children pressure them to buy brand-name or otherwise popular toys, games, and foods, nearly 80 percent of them answered "never" or "rarely." Another 17 percent answered "not very much."

Granted, turning the set off (or simply disposing of it) may be a difficult proposition for some families, or at least for some family members. But, as I have said, there was life before TV, and it was a life of riches that many of us have now at least partially forgotten, although they are not altogether gone. As TV-free families can attest, the local library is actually not a dusty, boring old building. The garden—the work it requires and the satisfactions it brings—offers pleasures and a sense of connectedness that the flickering of the TV screen cannot match. Giving free rein to our creativity—designing, building, doing artwork, writing, letting our imaginations roam—sustains us: it nourishes our souls. The silence itself that settles in when the TV leaves the house quickly comes to seem comfortingly familiar, and it has no commercial agenda whatsoever. In fact, TV-free families were clearly managing to thrive without being told what to do, buy, eat, drink, wear, or drive or how to enjoy themselves. In their estimation, turning off the set was a small price to pay.

4: how to
miss nothing

> *Life isn't perfect without TV, and we still have plenty of things to argue about. It's just that who's holding the remote isn't one of them.*
> **—TV-free survey participant**

In view of the prominent position television occupies in our lives and our homes, as well as the consumerism that drives our economy and our culture, it is hardly surprising that we're encouraged to be sure we have the right set for the right place. There are pocket TVs, waterproof TVs, and swivel models for the kitchen, as well as flip-down models for our cars, durable, neon-colored sets for the children, and huge plasma screens equipped with surround sound that can transform the living room into a theatre filled with light and action and noise. Under such circumstances, a person who chooses to forgo television can easily seem like a renegade—someone who perversely refuses to get with the program. Perhaps this explains why those in the mainstream (that is, TV watchers) are often convinced that people who don't have television must be missing something.

So what did the twelve hundred men, women, and children who responded to my TV-free survey say they were missing when the TV was turned off? Basically, nothing. The consensus was that life isn't lived on a screen—that the hours we spend actively engaged in something or with someone are far more fulfilling than hours spent staring at the TV. Most of these people had gone for years without a television in their home; some had lived their entire life without it. The four and a half hours a day that might have been lost to the set offered countless possibilities for more satisfying forms of recreation—for good leisure. As these TV-free individuals were quick to point out, these alternative pursuits often brought unanticipated benefits to themselves, to their families, and even to their communities.

After Don and Beth[*] got rid of their TV, they started having more dinners and get-togethers with their friends. "It's as though we rekindled the lost art of conversation," they reported. Something as simple as eating a meal together and talking was, they discovered, great entertainment in itself. Without a video to occupy them, the kids took to inventing their own games, sometimes quite elaborate ones, that they played contentedly for hours. Don and Beth found that they could keep up with current affairs and the sports news by listening to the radio—which meant that, if they needed to, they could get something else done at the same time. They planted a raised-bed garden and wallpapered the rooms in their home, and Beth learned to sew in order to make window coverings. "We rarely did such things before." Beth commented. "There was never time because we all had our favorite programs."

"We placed the TV in a closet one spring to see whether we could survive for a few weeks," another couple recalled. "The first day we gathered in the living room and realized we were sitting on the couch facing a blank wall. We moved everything around to facilitate conversation and reading. The other half of our living room now holds a card table for puzzles, games, and sewing. I went to the library for the first time in months, and we've been digging out old albums to listen to music we haven't played in years. We were surprised how easy the transition was, and we really enjoy the peace and quiet that TV-free life brings."

In Chad's estimation, his family enjoyed much more unstructured, "creative" time after the TV was removed from the household. Because dinners and evening commitments had often been scheduled around favorite shows and news programs, turning off the set gave his family a welcome sense of amplitude, as though their days had suddenly become longer. Marvin and June, a couple from Union Bridge, Maryland, commented: "We talk more. We accomplish more. We think more. We play more. We learn more. We live life rather than watch it. We spend more time sharing our lives." These and hundreds of other TV-free individuals were pleasantly surprised at how quickly the space formerly occupied by television became filled with far more

[*] Here and throughout the book, names have been changed to protect the privacy of survey participants.

memorable pursuits—so much so that some of them were embarrassed to think that they had lived so long just sitting and watching.

Replacements for Television   Many of my survey respondents recalled that, when they first gave up TV, they typically reached for "quick fixes," that is, some sort of temporary distraction or on-the-spot replacement for television. Reading a magazine or book, going for a walk or a bike ride, putting on some music, calling a friend on the phone, relaxing with a cup of tea, writing a letter, playing cards or a board game, listening to a book on tape, visiting with a neighbor, cleaning out an overstuffed closet or tidying a drawer, trying out a new recipe, doing a jigsaw puzzle, or even just taking a nap—these were only a few of the ad hoc pursuits that were mentioned. Even when they produced little by way of concrete gains, these quick fixes brought people a sense of satisfaction and often yielded an unexpected byproduct: time for reflection.

The first day of going TV free, Barbara sat down and made a long list of all the little things she never seemed to have time to do. In addition to certain chores she had been putting off, her list included practicing a long-neglected instrument, writing to her grandmother, and soaking in a hot bath. Whenever it was time for a favorite program to come on, she simply looked at the list of alternatives and went down it, check, check, check. On some days she accomplished more than she did on others, but she was thrilled finally to be getting to things that had for so long been postponed. Robin, a stay-at-home mother, simply decided to go for a walk whenever it was time for one of her favorite sitcoms to come on. She lost twenty pounds in one year. Another mother, Sarah, had been in the habit of setting her toddler, Connor, in front of the TV while she did housework. One day, as a quick fix, she decided to arrange a safe spot in the kitchen for Connor, where she could keep an eye on him while he played. It worked. Connor soon learned to entertain himself by finding objects hidden in a large plastic container of rice, by cutting up pieces of paper with child scissors, or by measuring out cups of flour and sugar for his mother's recipes.

Even those of us who are well accustomed to the TV-free life sometimes need a quick fix. Several years ago, I had a late-afternoon class to teach for twelve weeks, and so I needed care for my six- and ten-year-olds for two extra hours on Wednesdays. It occurred to me that a video or two would fill the bill—if we had a television, which we didn't. I was tempted just to leave them on their own, as there were always books and projects underway, until I thought of Bea, an elderly neighbor of ours who was also a painter. I did not want to impose, but I needed a solution, and using the television as a babysitter was not an option.

As I debated whether to phone Bea, a deep memory clicked in, and I remembered visiting an elderly neighbor, Mary King, when I was a child. She was very old, and she was confined to a wheelchair. Several times a week, I would walk a half mile down the road to visit her. I was not doing this to be nice so much as to play on her footstool and assist her in moving her electric bed up and down. Mary also fed me great snacks, the most memorable of which was a delicious chunk of "condensed" angel food cake—one that had fallen. I recalled how tears would come into the eyes of her husband, Jim, when he told stories of my visits with Mary long after she was gone. I thought about how often opportunities to know others are lost because children stay home and entertain themselves with television.

So I called Bea, who was delighted by the idea, and a Wednesday routine began. After school, my kids packed a snack, traipsed through the woods to Bea's house, did their homework, painted pictures with her, entertained her with the latest elementary school gossip, and had an all-round good time. My daughter brought along her little dog, Peter Pan, so that he and Bea's dog, Bennie, could romp together. I will ever be grateful for the twelve Wednesday afternoons my kids spent with Bea, and I have a feeling those times were very special for her, too. Quick-fix activities such as this one are not usually hard to find. Better yet, not only are they readily available, but the children, neighbors, pets, friends, and others who are involved in whatever the activity may be also reap the rewards.

Creativity and Self-Enrichment   The search for something—anything—to put in the place of television is a form of experimentation. It makes sense, then, that what begins as a quick fix can sometimes prove so enjoyable that it develops into a long-term, self-enriching hobby. Gardening, writing, woodworking, quilting, learning a musical instrument, keeping scrapbooks, playing sports, painting, and cooking, as well as a variety of book-related activities, were among the dozens of creative outlets that TV-free individuals discovered after the television was banished from the household. "I have more hobbies now, and I read more than I did during my TV-watching era," commented Candace, from Richmond, California. "I scrapbook, stencil, and cross-stitch. I have time to read the newspaper, and I've even written a few letters to the editor that got published. Now I have time to sit outside, enjoy my yard, and watch my toddler play."

Realizing that he was addicted to television, Stan tried putting his television in the basement with only a hard metal folding chair in front of it. After a few weeks of trudging down the stairs, he figured it wasn't worth it. Instead, he decided to try building model boats, just for fun. His boys quickly became intrigued as well, and thus a shared hobby was born. Stacy cancelled her cable subscription and discovered that instead of watching all the quilting, cooking, home improvement, gardening, and woodworking shows available twenty-four hours a day on cable channels, she was now actually quilting, cooking, and making improvements to her garden and home. She was happy, she said, to be able to spend the $30.80 monthly cable fee on her new recreational pursuits.

TV-free parents also described some of the creative solutions to boredom that their children devised. Eight-year-old Alan spent several days building traps for bugs. Five-year-old Sylvia set up "school" at the same time each day for all her stuffed animals, complete with paper, crayons, and treats for those who answered questions correctly. Then there was four-year-old Alisa, who was addicted to Disney's *The Little Mermaid*. "Alisa had watched the Disney video once or twice a day for several months, loved it, and had it practically memorized," her mother wrote. "When we decided to try life without TV, I was worried about how she might react. The first thirty minutes she wandered around the house, whining about missing her friends from *The Little Mermaid*. Within an hour, though, I discovered her slithering all over the place in whatever mermaid outfits she could dream up (mostly my silky nightgowns), singing every single *Little Mermaid* song she knew, lost in her own fantasy world. I imagine the scenes she made up were even better than the movie!"

Children were also called upon to do chores and, as many TV-free families reported, were quite capable of inventing long, fantastic stories to tell to each other while doing so. Washing dishes or loading the dishwasher, picking tomatoes or green beans from the garden, pitting cherries, setting the table, tidying up a bedroom, stemming grapes for juice, vacuuming the floors, podding peas—helping out with household tasks gives children a sense of accomplishment, as well as offering scope for interaction with each other or with a parent. Similarly, play activities such as constructing a snow fort, listening to a book on tape and acting out the stories, teaching spelling to stuffed animals, making mud pies, or turning couch cushions into fantasy houses are enriching for children because they involve physical action or imagination, or both. These creative forms of play provide opportunities for communication, problem solving (generally by trial and error), cooperation, and the development of motor skills. Of course, all children engage in such activities, but TV-free children engage in them more often because they have more time in which to do so.

Adolescents who had grown up in TV-free households tended to have definite insights into how their lives had been shaped without the constant influence of television. Joy, from Smalley, Wisconsin, felt that the absence of a TV set was largely responsible for her love of books as well as for her interest in writing, baking, and playing piano—pursuits that her TV-free parents had "forced" her to discover. She remembered how the vivid games of make-believe she had played as a child had fed her imaginative life. And, she added, "I also think that without TV, the media has much less effect on the way I feel about my body and how I look." During the Winter Olympics in 2000, and again in 2006, two-time silver medalist Bode Miller talked about the impact of being brought up without TV. Obliged to design his own entertainment, he threw his extra hours a day into skiing. Tennis champions Bob and Mike Ryan were also raised without television. "It helped us," Mike commented in an interview, "because it gave us more time to work on our studies and practice. Now we're thankful."[1] My teenage son says he owes his skill in soccer and the success of his rock 'n' roll band to living without television: growing up, he spent his spare time training or practicing the guitar.

Getting Involved As weeks, months, and eventually years passed by without TV, many of those surveyed made long-term commitments to their new interests, with the result that former quick fixes eventually evolved beyond hobbies into serious, life-transforming pursuits. Some started out bowling, skiing, walking, swimming, or weight training and, like Bode Miller and the Ryans, wound up entering sports competitions. Journal writing gave way to professional writing, of fiction and of nonfiction. One of my respondents said he began going for bike rides instead of watching television, then became interested in bicycle racing, and ended up with a job in bicycle repair. Others became skilled in woodworking, fly-tying, gardening, music, or photography, while yet others went back to college or graduate school or undertook some sort of specialized training. In short, changes in basic life patterns from passive to active variously resulted in improved fitness or the acquisition of new skills, as well as, in many cases, an expansion of an individual's ways of thinking and perceiving.

Community involvement was often a natural sequel to this broadening of horizons. After removing television from their lives, many of the study participants gravitated toward groups of one sort or another. People who had never imagined taking a decision-making role in their communities were surprised to find themselves serving as board members, club officers, or volunteer coordinators. Some joined, or even founded, special-interest groups. They became involved in childcare or food cooperatives, book clubs, or gourmet cooking classes, activities that required weekly or monthly commitments. Some of these organizations addressed themselves directly to community needs and local issues; others were more in the nature of clubs or hobby groups. But whatever the specific activity, turning off the TV set frequently sparked a newfound desire to get out of the house and connect with other people—to replace virtual reality with the genuine thing.

Following a divorce, James had only weekends with his children. He soon realized how much of this all-too-brief time they spent just sitting around watching television, and so he decided to get rid of his TV set. The kids rebelled at first, but it was only a few weeks before a more satisfying routine developed. They went to parks, had conversations, played board games, cooked meals together, and sometimes went to the movies. Finding himself without a television, James also discovered that he had extra time during the week and decided to join a local volunteer program that had been established to revitalize the downtown community in his area. Not long after joining, he headed up a fund-raising effort that eventually resulted in the construction of a multimillion-dollar performing arts center. In answer to a question about the most important changes that giving up television had produced, James said that the biggest consequence was his increased community involvement. Working for the public good brought him a great deal of pleasure and a sense of personal fulfillment—music to the ears of those of us who work in the field of recreation and community development.

Several of the TV-free adolescents who participated in the study reported that what had begun as hobbies were developing into possible careers. At the age of fifteen, Tom was so proficient at Web design that he was already getting contracts for his creative work. At twelve, Jenny was designing and sewing American Doll clothes and had her own loyal customers. One eleven-year-old girl had already entered two poetry contests, written several essays for a fledgling book, and produced a one-page school newsletter. Regardless of the long-term uses to which their talents might be put, their success gave them something to be proud of—and people rarely take pride in having sat all evening in front of the TV.

The Greatest Show on Earth "Remember all of those things that you'd like to do with your kids," one TV-father remarked, "but you just never have the time? Well, you do have the time. You're just using it for something that has absolutely no lasting value, whereas time spent actually doing things with children has tremendous lasting value." So, we could add, does spending time with yourself, or with friends and neighbors, or with just about anybody else. Much has been written about how "screen time," that is, the hours we devote to watching TV or playing video games or entertaining ourselves at the computer, tends not only to distort our perceptions but even to undermine our fundamental connection to reality. We are tempted to accept the world presented to us on screens—a world that is often highly

living outside the box

idealized or otherwise heavily contrived—as our image of "normal," and then we define ourselves in relation to it. Rather than drawing the map ourselves, we let others draw it for us. And we grow accustomed to engaging with that world, which comes to seem safer and more comfortable than the sometimes challenging situations we encounter in our daily lives. Submerge yourself in a fantasy world often enough, and ordinary, concrete events can begin to seem trivial and intrusive.

The advent of "reality" shows may be the ultimate irony. In an interview about *Frontline*'s "The Merchants of Cool," consulting producer Douglas Rushkoff noted that the kids who appear on MTV's *The Reality Show* have grown up watching MTV and have modeled their behavior accordingly. So, he argues, "when MTV takes a bunch of them and puts them in a house and puts a camera on them, they're not putting a camera on the real world. They are photographing people who've been programmed how to behave by MTV. So where is the reality in the equation?"[2] The idea that reality is something presented to us on television offers a somewhat chilling commentary on our own lives. "Once upon a time," writes John Monczunski, "people socialized by interacting, playing cards, chatting. Now, more than likely, they sit together and silently watch a TV program, ironically, sometimes of people having a conversation."[3]

Who, then, is missing what? Suppose we were to take only *one* of the however-many hours we currently dedicate to television each day. That would give us 365 hours in the course of a year—more than 45 eight-hour days. Think how much better we would know our children if we spent that time talking or playing with them—or how much better we might get to know ourselves. Think how our friends and neighbors might benefit from our company or what we might accomplish for the community. And imagine how very different our collective experience might be if we spent not one but *all* of those hours immersed in our own lives rather than the world served up to us on TV.

5: the decision to go tv free

We haven't watched TV for more than sixteen years, not out of a need to make a statement against society or because of any overt religious injunction, but because of a simple desire to have more time for a meaningful marriage and family in the face of a busy life.

—TV-free father
from Smalley, Wisconsin

As I read through the hundreds of pages of written comments supplied by the women and men who responded to my survey, I was struck by how many of them reported that they felt quite alone in their decision to give up television. Relatively few, I realized, were aware of another person or family who had made a similar commitment. But then even I had been caught off guard by the response to my initial ads: evidently I had underestimated the size of the TV-free population. Although many of my respondents had lived without television for years, they seemed surprised, as well as pleased, to learn that someone had an interest in the choice they had made—in their decision to take the "road less traveled."

In retrospect, their sense of isolation is perfectly understandable. Our culture is saturated with television. It takes real courage for a lone adult to swim against the tide, and it requires even greater courage for parents to ban the television from the family gathering place (to say nothing of their children's bedrooms). Choosing to give up television thus requires a certain fortitude, a willingness to embrace the spirit of rugged individualism in a society that pressures us to conform. But if the decision to go

TV free can seem a lonely one, the overwhelming majority—nearly nine out of ten—of my respondents said it was a choice they never regretted. At least after the first couple of weeks, life without television turned out not to be the hardship that some of them had feared it would be. Far from feeling deprived, they were excited to discover that there were many other ways to spend their leisure time—activities that, as we have seen, were not only enjoyable but brought them a refreshing sense of genuine satisfaction. This is not to say they always had an easy time of it. As Kristen commented, "TV-free adults aren't saints. They've struggled with dissension and backsliding." But the fact that they hung in there suggests that something about life without television seemed worth the fight.

For some of the roughly seven hundred adults who responded to the survey questionnaire, the decision to turn off the set was a spontaneous one, triggered by a specific, even comical, event. For others, the desire to create a life centered around something other than the TV set was rooted in resentments and memories of childhood neglect. For yet others, not watching television was simply a habit they had developed over the years, while yet others had grown up without TV and had never acquired a taste for it. Ultimately, of course, each individual or couple had arrived at their TV-free lifestyle by their own route. Even so, it was apparent that their decision was often motivated by one of five broad reasons: (1) a moment of truth or turning point, frequently spurred by marriage or parenthood, (2) resentment over childhood experiences with television or frustration with the programming itself, (3) "technical difficulties"—that is, problems with reception or a situation that temporarily disabled the TV set, (4) some sort of outside influence or prompting, such as National TV-Turnoff Week or a book about the harmful effects of television, and (5) growing up in a TV-free household.

Turning Points

■ In the middle of a Monday night football game, Dennis's two-year-old son put a book under his dad's nose and said, "Read me." Here was a very young child with a very simple request, fully trusting that it would be met. Dennis looked into his son's face and slowly rose to turn off the TV.

- Years ago, Wendy was sitting on the floor with her infant son watching *Oprah* when she suddenly realized she was paying far more attention to the show than to her new baby. That evening, she and her husband decided to get rid of the TV. "We have *never* regretted it," she said.
- Bev's husband gave the TV away the year they married. "He's a total zombie in front of it," Bev reported. "We would have had to change his name to 'Andy Damn-it-turn-it-off Smith' if we'd kept it!"
- Amy and Greg also decided to go TV free just before they got married and were brave enough to announce their decision to others. It caused quite a stir among family members, one of whom, undeterred, presented them with a widescreen TV as a wedding gift.
- In their previous marriages, both Connie and Dave had ended up watching far more TV than they would have liked: "It was a way for two people who didn't want to talk to each other to kill time." When they married, they vowed to do without this electronic interloper.
- Pam and her husband jettisoned their TV in April 1990 so that they could concentrate on finishing their respective master's degrees. "It was harder for me because I had certain favorite shows," Pam wrote. "But after three weeks, the weather got to be far too nice outside to sit in front of a TV inside. By the fall, we were reading, woodworking, and even socializing with our neighbors." Her advice: "Toss your television in the spring."

Dennis admitted that he was completely wrapped up in the Monday football game he was watching and was quite taken aback when a children's book suddenly blocked the screen from view. "What else could I do?" he commented. Wendy, too, had quite an epiphany when she caught herself shushing her child's cooing so that she could hear Oprah's interview. Megan, a young mother whose husband was a helicopter pilot in the National Guard, recalled an incident that took place that during the First Persian Gulf War. When news footage showed a helicopter being blown out of the sky, her toddler pointed to the screen and cried "Dada!" Megan turned the set off and reassured her daughter, but over the next several days the footage was shown repeatedly. Finally, after a night of soul searching, she carried the TV out the back door and heaved it into the dumpster.

Many other young parents relayed similar experiences, in which a specific event, sometimes a seemingly minor one, suddenly brought them up short and caused them to reassess their priorities. This "moment of clarity" allowed them to put the initial sacrifice of their own favorite programs into the proper perspective. The same process applied to the fringe benefits of having a television. Jan remembered, somewhat ruefully, how the living room used to stay neater a lot longer when her children spent much of their time in front of the TV. Ruth recalled the leisurely hot showers she used to enjoy while her two toddlers were entertained with *Teletubbies*. "I'd be a cleaner mom with TV," she laughed, "but hey, that's what one gets for being proactive!" Again and again, TV-free parents declared that, in the greater scheme of things, the loss of such "perks" was trivial. Next to the emotional and developmental needs of one's children, a tidy living room is poor competition.

As Amy and Greg's experience illustrates, friends and family are not always prepared to respect the wishes of the TV free: the widescreen wedding gift still arrived. The fact is that owning a television (or, rather, several) is the social norm, and when someone chooses to depart from a norm, other people often feel uncomfortable. Another young couple, Nolan and Raylene, reported that some of their friends teased them constantly about their lack of a TV and even seemed in some way threatened by their decision. Both couples mentioned that, on occasion, a friend or relative actually snooped through the house to see whether they were telling the truth. Acquaintances also tended to predict, with a certain degree of self-satisfaction, that the TV-free couple would break down and buy the big-screen babysitter once children arrived. One woman described how her husband's brother had urged them to reconsider their decision, arguing quite vehemently that their two-year-old daughter would be "too different" from her peers without a TV in the household—that it would be "traumatic." With a twinkle in his eye, her husband replied, "You mean traumatic for the other kids, because she's so much smarter and way more creative?"

Over the years, a number of these TV-free adults had received offers of cast-off TVs from friends who were upgrading. One couple reported that a friend of theirs, hearing that they no longer had a television, and having evidently failed to grasp the idea, promptly told them, "Oh, there's a special on TVs this week at Wal-Mart!" TV-free couples were often asked, "What do you do with all that time?" or "Was this an intentional decision?" Or acquaintances would comment, "I wish I could do that"— although, as Raylene remarked, "When I tell them that they, too, can do this, their eyes often glaze over." Glen said that he sometimes feels as if he's back in high school, standing on the outside of an in-group defined by a devotion to television. He also recalled that, in his TV-watching days, he used to laugh when he saw famous people being interviewed who seemed clueless about what was on television. "I realize now that they were too busy living life to spend much time observing it from the sidelines," he commented.

Another couple noted that, even after a dozen years, many of their friends still insist they're "missing out" by not owning a TV. Yet, they said, they have never doubted their decision. "We find that our time together is more meaningful and intense, not because we *have* to interact with each other, but because we *choose* to," Mary wrote. "My heart goes out to couples who miss the intimacy of long chats in the evenings. We're almost never in a hurry, and that has had a tremendous positive impact on my stress level. Years ago, when I regularly watched TV, I could burn hours away gazing at the glowing phosphors, and I always ended up missing the important things." Many of my married respondents had chosen partners who already shared their values, but in some cases one spouse had converted the other, generally without much difficulty. Couples typically reported that the period of withdrawal was less difficult than they had anticipated and that the benefits were not only noticeable immediately but far outweighed any sense of loss over the sacrifice of certain programs.

The results of the survey suggest that these couples made a wise choice. The adults represented in the study spent, on average, 48 minutes a day in "meaningful conversation" with their spouse, and over 80 percent agreed that being TV free contributed to a stronger marriage. As if to underscore the point, according to a January 18, 2006, news report on National Public Radio, a research study conducted in Italy discovered that couples who had a television in their bedroom made love only half as often as couples without one. For individuals over the age of fifty, the difference was even more striking: couples who had a TV in the bedroom reported only one intimate episode a month, on average, whereas those without had seven. And if keeping television out of the bedroom is apparently a good thing, keeping it out of the house altogether may be even better. My own survey found that couples who lived without a television in their home made love an average of twelve times a month, or about three times a week.[1] Not that getting rid of the TV will guarantee a better sex life, but chances are it won't hurt.

Resentment and Frustration ▪ Robin remembers her father coming home on the 5:32 train every evening, fixing a couple of martinis, and unwinding, alone, in front of the TV.

- Greg was raised by a single mother who was addicted to soap operas. She taped any she had to miss. Jan's father was a truck driver, who was often gone for weeks at a time. He also came home to the TV and didn't want to be bothered. Bill said that when he was a kid, his parents planned every evening around certain favorite shows.

- Don tired of watching a major news story take an entire day to unfold on CNN. He knew he could get more insightful coverage by spending a few minutes with the BBC Web page.

- Twenty years ago, Paula heard Phyllis Schlafly speak on a talk show. Paula was so enraged by Schlafly's antifeminist views that she threw a book at the TV screen and broke it.

- Liz and Sadie (who live in two different states) trashed their respective TVs when the popular show *Thirtysomething* was cancelled. One of them felt it was the last good show on television; the other wrote to the network to complain.

- One night, when neither her husband nor her two small children would listen when she told them to come to dinner, Jenny grabbed the garden shears and cut the TV cable out by the utility pole. She still remembers the shrieks of horror that resounded from the house. Now, years later, the kids are fourteen and twenty, and the TV set is history.

- The evening Grace left her husband, he was watching television, as he had been for many years leading up to that moment. She spoke softly. He turned the volume down. She told him she could not live with him anymore. He nodded and turned back to the TV.

Resorting to the garden shears may be somewhat extreme, but Jenny realized that sooner or later her volcano of frustration had to blow. With three TVs in the house, no one talked anymore. Lives were scheduled around the news and favorite programs. Dinner was eaten in shifts, usually in the company of the TV. Jenny's children were tucked away in their rooms all evening, watching television or playing video games. Following her spontaneous decision to cut the cable, she reported, life hardly became a bed of roses overnight. Her five-year-old son sobbed that he missed his TV "f-f-friends," while her husband sat silently in the living room, the remote at his elbow, and their two daughters disappeared over to friends' homes to watch their favorite shows. Slowly, though, the initial upheaval gave way to calm. The kids discovered all sorts of other things to do, and dinner was transformed into a pleasant, and uninterrupted, family ritual. The art of conversation was resurrected, and lively discussions replaced the numbed silence of sitcom-watching. Even Jenny's husband came around. "At least now I know as much about my own kids as I used to know about *The Simpsons*," he conceded. Jenny still stays in touch, and in a recent email she wrote: "Until people realize that letting their kids watch life instead of living it is tantamount to letting Paris Hilton and The Donald raise their children, the upcoming generation is doomed to become so many uncultured couch potatoes."

In addition to sheer frustration with the apparent omnipotence of the television set, many adults still harbored bitterness over their own upbringing, feeling that, as children, they had come in second to the box. Lynn remembered having to listen to boring adult conversations in which the dominant topic was television and its pantheon of stars. Now parents themselves, these individuals hoped that raising their own children without television would spare them the same experience of neglect. Alice, for example, felt that she had basically been raised by the TV. Some of her earliest memories involved situation comedies and soap operas. The sound of the television had become her pathology of normalcy, and, after she married, she and her husband kept the set on constantly. Even when they weren't actually watching it, the television was there in the background. When Alice became pregnant, she began to give serious consideration to the choices she would make as a parent. She knew she was unhappy about her own upbringing. Her parents hadn't seemed interested in her or in the rest of the family, and she felt that her own communication skills and her ability to deal with life's realities were underdeveloped as a result. "One of the few things I could control," she said, "was the influence TV would have on my child."

Largely because of social pressure, however, getting rid of the TV proved to be something of a trial. For one thing, both she and her husband had to contend with a stream of negative feedback from nearly everyone they knew. Moreover, even after they had sold their TV, Alice's mother continued to insist that her grandchild would be "deprived." So, as a surprise, she purchased a small TV with a built-in VCR, which she unveiled in the baby's room. Another TV-free father complained that when he and his wife and child visit his folks, his dad invariably greets his young grandson at the door grinning broadly, with an armful of videos for the boy to watch. As Rose put it, "It seems as if, when we reject TV, my parents feel we are rejecting them as well because TV is where they get most of their social interaction."

Rose's observation raises an important consideration. Even the best decisions aren't necessarily made for the best reasons. When a grown child remains angry at his or her parents for apparently valuing television more than they did their own children, and so resolves not to perpetuate the crime, this resentment may very well communicate itself to the parents. The grown child is essentially saying, "Look—I'm not going to do to my children what you did to me." In such cases, the now-grandparents may pick up on the tacit accusation and react defensively. A grandfather who proffers videos when he knows full well that his son's household is TV free is either remarkably insensitive or else is caught up in a tug-of-war with his son. Similarly, while it could be that someone like Alice's mother is merely arrogant—convinced that she's right and determined to have her own way—it could also be that she senses the criticism implicit in her child's decision and so feels hurt or threatened. Even when the resentment is justified, pent-up anger has a way of poisoning relationships. Perhaps, then, parents who decide to raise their own children without TV need to reflect on their motives and make an effort to avoid sending a message of blame to their own parents.

For others, anger had to do not with memories of their own upbringing but with the vast wasteland of television itself. A number of my respondents pointed to time wasted on nonstop news coverage as a deciding factor. "I would flip through the channels," Sheila recalled, describing how she ended up a news junkie, "and realized nothing interested me. I even watched the TV guide channel! The last straw was the latest media blitz—you know, the crisis of the moment. Each channel showed the exact same scenario, play by play, over and over again. Then all the newscasters and 'experts' gave their opinions on the scenario over and over. I decided at that point that I had more positive things to do with my life than sit passively and waste my time on depressing images repeated way beyond my control. I would rather talk to a real human being about events, good or bad."

During the 1990–91 war in the Persian Gulf, Lance and his wife found themselves watching two or three hours of mind-numbing news coverage every night after work. "After two weeks," Lance said, "we cancelled cable and never looked back." My husband and I, who were already TV free when the war began, borrowed a TV so that we could keep up with the news. We soon began to feel that unless we were familiar, in minute detail, with all the latest developments and could recite the most recent casualty figures, we were out of touch. It was the one and only time we ever considered breaking down and buying a set, although we eventually lost interest in the idea. As we later realized, however, incessant news reporting, with its tacit suggestion that you aren't informed unless you're overinformed, had nearly seduced us into backsliding.

Like many others who found themselves married to a TV addict, Esther put up with a diet of several hours of TV, night after night, for a great many years. More than one of my survey respondents regretfully admitted that they had accepted such a situation until a separation or divorce ensued. It wasn't until they found themselves single again that they realized what a huge part of their own lives TV had become. On the one hand, the television offered much-needed companionship, of sorts, now that they were on their own—a comforting sense of the familiar. On the other hand, it discouraged contact with the outside world and the pursuit of other interests. In the wake of a separation, they were faced with yet another choice: whether to continue to spend their evenings watching television or attempt to give it up.

When Esther and her son moved out, she chose not to have a television. She was surprised when it turned out that her son—who used to be upset if he missed a favorite show—didn't particularly mourn its loss. He said he liked having more time and being more physically active and declared that he felt "really free." For Grace, the choice was also clear. "I realized that the time I had spent watching TV, all those hours, days, and even years, was wasted time," she wrote. "I treasured all the books I had read, the family vacations, and playdates with other young parents, but memories of watching TV were one big black hole." Many of those who left a TV-addicted spouse made an effort to pursue other activities, including those that got them out of the house and involved in groups. They spoke of the differences they saw in their new relationships, the time outdoors they now enjoyed, the fact that they had more experiences they could genuinely cherish, and even of their growing ability to be comfortable sitting quietly and alone. As their own horizons widened and they began to feel happier and more fulfilled, the resentment they felt at having had a spouse who was basically married to the TV often receded.

Technical Difficulties

- On September 5, 1996, Hurricane Fran plunged Lisa's home into darkness. After several days without a working TV, her kids convinced her to get rid of it for good.
- Shortly after Marie and her husband brought their baby daughter home, their TV conked out. "We were so busy, we didn't miss it. Later, we realized how much it sapped our time."
- After the family's TV broke down, Gina's oldest daughter wanted her father to fix it and even offered him $25 to make the repairs.

However, after a few days of music, games, and outdoor activities, she found herself outnumbered by her three siblings, who voted for throwing the set out. They were getting more attention from their parents than they had before, and they wanted it to stay that way.

- One young couple insisted that their initial decision to go without TV was motivated not by any sort of enlightened thinking but purely by the need to cut costs. "We disconnected cable service to save money when I became ill carrying our second child and had to stop working. Life was so drastically different without the TV, and the change in our four-year-old son was so positive, that we decided never to turn it on again."

Hurricanes, ice storms, floods, and other natural disasters can cause staggering amounts of damage, and their effects can be deeply traumatic. But when the worst that results is a blackout, the consequences can be rather pleasant. Time slows down, and neighbors help each other out. Hot dogs are roasted over an open fire, and dinners eaten by candlelight. Water is heated by a propane stove, and families wash dishes together. And, of course, the TV stops working.

As Lisa and her family discovered, a temporary loss of power can be the first step in the decision to go TV free. When Hurricane Fran left them without television for several days, the net result was far more family interaction. Board games were brought out, she recalled, and she and her husband entertained the children with stories. In the end, it was the kids who begged for the set to be discarded. Gina's children reacted in much the same way: life without television just seemed to be more fun. Having a newborn in the house kept Marie and her husband pretty well occupied when their TV broke. "The first week really was the hardest," Marie reported. "But then we were so pleased with all the extra time, and with the quality of that time, we decided to become TV free." Like many other couples and families, once they'd had a taste of togetherness, they didn't want to go back.

Survey respondents also had plenty of stories to tell about cable television. Quite a few reported having moved to an area where reception was poor, which meant that in order to continue watching television they would have to subscribe to cable. Faced with the choice, they had decided not to bother with it. Others were annoyed by the high cost of cable service. A number of newlywed couples, in particular, had been willing to give the low-to-no TV life a try in exchange for a savings of $30 to $50 a month. What began as a desire to economize often led to the recognition that alternatives to television abound and that life without TV is full of unexpected, and inexpensive, riches.

Maggie moved from a home in which the television barely received anything to a new house already equipped with cable. More than anyone else in the family, Maggie wanted to keep the cable service. She had fallen in love with the Home and Garden Channel and could sit for hours absorbing new decorating and gardening ideas. Occasionally, she would put one of them into practice, but she was aware that she was spending a great deal of time just watching. Although reading had long been a pastime for the entire family, the habit of sitting down with a book dropped away dramatically in their new home, what with the wide variety of network and cable programs now available. It seemed inevitable to Maggie that soon everyone would have his or her own favorite channel, as she herself did. So, for the sake of the family as a whole, Maggie decided to stop the cable service. Without it, the reception was once again very poor, and soon not only cable (and its cost) but network TV as well were a thing of the past. As if by magic, reading reemerged as a favorite pastime.

Outside Prompts

- Louella turned off the television in 1973, when she enrolled her six- and eight-year-old children at the Waldorf school in Garden City, New York. Waldorf schools strongly advocate TV-free households.
- Tara was going through a divorce, and television was her preferred babysitter, until her three children brought home a note from school about National TV-Turnoff Week.
- Gary wrote a research paper for a college class in which he examined the evidence linking TV viewing and violence. That was enough to convert him.
- In Peter's case, as in several others, a book about the negative effects of television proved to be the driving force behind the decision to try the TV-free life.

A number of parents who participated in the survey were great supporters of Waldorf schools. Located all across the country, Waldorf schools take the impact of TV on the lives of children very seriously and recommend that parents get rid of their TVs, at least while their children are enrolled in the school. Louella, who is today a grandmother, remains grateful for the experience. "The creativity, values, ability to listen, enthusiasm, and zest for life my children have demonstrated are far deeper, compared to so many in their age group, who grew up hypnotized by the electronic box," she wrote. "Their values are now utterly their own, their perspective incredibly wise for their years, and the balance they maintain a blessing to their spouses and offspring. I credit a great deal of this to the absence of television in their most formative years." Of course, this is a parent speaking, but her obvious pride in her children is enough to suggest that a decision she made thirty years ago has indeed had its legacy, one that now extends to the next generation. Waldorf parents also repeatedly commented that, quite apart from the multiple benefits to their children, the sense of camaraderie they felt with other Waldorf parents was a real advantage when they first tried life without TV.

Thousands of other schools encourage families to observe National TV-Turnoff Week, which celebrated its twelfth year in 2006. Sponsored by the Center for Screen-Time Awareness, based in Washington, D.C., National TV-Turnoff Week takes place in the last week of April. During that time, we are urged to take a break from television and evaluate its role in our lives and in the lives of our children. Over the years, millions of people have spent a week discovering what free time can be when it isn't held hostage to television.

When Tara's children brought home the slip of paper asking parents to become involved in TV-Turnoff Week, she did not welcome the challenge. "With my marriage ending—the separation and the transition from married, stay-at-home mom to divorced, working mom—I couldn't bear to part with my electronic babysitter!" she recalled. Her kids were eager to take part, however, so she decided to give it a try. Reluctantly, she covered the TV with a towel and steeled herself for the first day. But her worries soon dissipated. Rather than complaining or moping around, as she had feared they would, her children simply played. Nor were there the standard squabbles about whether they would be allowed to watch "one more show" or about the need to switch off the TV and come to dinner. As Tara went on to explain:

My mind felt fresher and less cluttered each day the TV was turned off. So I decided near the end of TV-Turnoff Week to make it permanent. I called the cable company and told them to disconnect. Without cable, we get no reception whatsoever. I put the TV in a closet and braced myself for the children's reactions. They didn't holler and fuss like I expected them to. Over the next couple of weeks, they continued to play, imagine things, and pretend. It was like they had their childhoods back, and we all felt relieved. I felt a tremendous amount of guilt lift. Now I'm more energized as a mother without TV. I hated the power struggles about how much to watch and when to turn it off. I am still challenged as a divorced mom, but my life is easier without TV. And I am the *last* one who would have thought that could happen!

In addition to TV-Turnoff Week, books about the negative influence of television frequently played a role in converting people to life outside the box. Survey participants repeatedly mentioned three in particular—Jerry Mander's *Four Arguments for the Elimination of Television*, Marie Winn's *The Plug-In Drug*, and the chapter on TV from Jim Trelease's *The Read-Aloud Handbook*. All are thoughtful, engaging reflections on the subject, and all provide solid arguments in favor of a life lived with little or no TV. Several of the participants remembered having read one of these books back when they were teenagers, in the course of writing a school report on the effects of television or as required reading for a college class. Sometimes the books had simply been passed along by friends, and they were often recommended to new parents.

Peter told this story about his "conversion by the book," which occurred nearly thirty-five years ago:

For several years after college, I picked apples at a family-run orchard in Vermont each fall. The pickers lived in communal housing on the back side of the property. There were about a dozen men and women, mostly young and free-spirited, and we had the choice of whether or not to keep a TV in the house. During my first season, the house was evenly divided, so the TV stayed right where it was, mounted on the table in the middle of the main living room. It was on early in the morning (*The Today Show*), during rain delays (*Tom and Jerry*), into the late afternoon (*Star Trek*) and early evening (*ABC World News*, with Peter Jennings), until we got off work. It droned on, demanding everyone's attention, until late at night when Mike, the crew insomniac, finally dozed off staring at the 3:00 a.m. static from a distant station in Quebec. Needless to say, the TV was annoying, and it weakened the collective vibe. After all, the only thing people were doing together in their free time was watching TV.

We had a different mix of people my second season. The first collective decision we made was to ditch the TV. The change was remarkable. People took turns preparing sumptuous meals that we shared in the main living room. Since there was no TV to click on, we sat around talking and laughing about the day's picking (or anything else that came to mind) as we let the meal settle in. Then, after the table was cleared and moved out of the way, and the dishes washed, we hacky-sacked together for another hour while my friend Sally baked round after round of chocolate chip cookies. Some of the pickers eventually drifted off to their rooms while others quietly read in the living room until bedtime. Then, one day, Sunny came back from the library with a book called *Four Arguments for the Elimination of Television* by a former ad executive named Jerry Mander. Sunny would occasionally burst out laughing and read aloud a passage from the book. I was intrigued and grabbed the book as soon as she was done.

In *Four Arguments*, Jerry Mander skillfully unveils how television colonizes our life experience, how its constant image stream diminishes our capacity for thought and reflection, how there are physiological reasons why it is so hypnotic, and how it is inherently autocratic and destroys democracy. It's a brilliant, well-argued book. At that moment, when my distaste for television was growing, it crystallized my thinking, and ever since I've strongly believed that a TV-free lifestyle is the much healthier way to go. Advice: Think of the moments in your life when you have been happiest and most at peace. I doubt you were sitting in front of a TV during those moments. Think of other things you really want to be doing. Make a list if you need to. Then, start doing them. Pretty soon, you won't have any time to waste with the tube!

Raised Without TV

- Devin grew up without a TV, and, at the age of thirty-two, he had this to say about television: "Whenever I watch some, I know again why we don't have one. It's a waste of time."
- May remembered the day her parents loaned their TV to an elderly neighbor whose set had broken. With the TV gone, May and what she called her "veteran couch potato" siblings actually started to play together. The second TV-free generation is now going strong.
- Gail always knew that, if she ever had children, she would raise them without TV. "I always thought my parents were very smart for not owning one" was her comment.
- Hannah spent most of her childhood without TV and still finds it hugely annoying. She and her husband opted to have a TV-free household, and with no regrets: "I think having no TV is the single most important child-rearing choice we've made."

Interestingly, those who had been raised without TV tended to be the most adamant and vocal about their decision to keep TV out of their homes as adults. They had been there. They knew that there were no socially devastating or otherwise life-threatening consequences for children who grow up without television, and they couldn't wait to raise their kids in the same manner. Yvonne, who described herself as a "reading addict" by the age of twelve, raved about the advantages of the TV-free approach: "We have a lively, not sedated, home, with plenty of things to argue about other than which show to watch." Devin remembered his parents encouraging him and his siblings to start hobbies or explore pursuits that might stay with them into adulthood and perhaps even someday earn them an income. He took up flying, his brother became interested in environmental issues, and a sister is now in the Peace Corps. When, on occasion, he finds himself in the presence of a TV, he is reminded of what he isn't missing. "I don't like the maniacal intensity of the conversation, particularly in the commercials," he commented, "and the fact that even an idiotic, unsatisfying show will suck in the attention of nearly everyone in the vicinity. I especially resent the loss of time for other, more satisfying activities." When May's parents realized that their four kids were off the couch, going outside, reading, and no longer asking for the latest junky cereals, the loan to the elderly neighbor whose set had broken became permanent. May remembered being impressed with the changes in her behavior and that of her siblings: "We all got really involved with active pursuits and never looked back." Now she can't imagine having even one hour to "give up" to TV: "I'm so busy with so many fun projects that I hardly have time to sit down!"

Gail has no memory of her family getting rid of the TV because it happened before she was three. What she does remember are afternoons wading in the creek with her sisters, playing hide-and-seek in her grandparents' hayloft, creeping quietly along the corridors of her neighbor's horse stalls, and playing house in the woods, an activity that involved the construction of elaborate and very functional tree houses. Twenty years later, neither Gail nor her siblings regret their parents' decision to forgo television. "Because we did not grow up honing our ability to tune out people in favor of listening to the television, and because we had more time in our day for conversation, each of us has matured into a compassionate 'people' person," Gail wrote. "Among human relationships, my sisters and I value family relationships the most. We are a tightly knit group, and both of my sisters were attendants in my recent wedding. Though none of us would deny the pleasures of wealth, we know the greatest happiness is brought by satisfying relationships, lifelong learning, giving and blessing others in some way. The giving comes from a combination of the values that our parents have instilled in us."

Kate's Decision   In some cases, the decision to stop watching television simply evolved naturally, over time, beginning with a vague curiosity about what such a life might be like and ultimately coming about in response to a more or less random combination of circumstances. Kate, a mother from Tennessee who was pregnant with her fourth child when the TV made its exit, took the time to share her story:

> I cannot honestly remember when or why it was we first started talking about getting rid of the television. I do remember making admiring comments about those families we'd heard about who had no television, although we hadn't actually met anyone. They seemed far off, not only in terms of distance but in life as well. No videos when the children are sick? No *Sesame Street* in the late afternoon, when you're tired and the kids are getting hungry? No taking breaks from the day to sit and escape to some other place—to someone else's life? No sitting, sitting, sitting, in front of the TV? What would we do all the time? That certainly wouldn't work at my house—at least not this week! But it sure was an interesting idea to consider.
>
> Then two families, friends of ours, switched off their TVs for good. In one family, the power had gone out for a week after a serious ice storm. They enjoyed stories by candlelight, cooking on the woodstove, and early bedtimes. They put the television in the closet, after the large black box sitting in the middle of the living room lost its magnetic appeal, and when the power came back on, they left it there. The funny thing was, it was weeks before the children noticed it was missing. The other family we knew just got tired of the violence, the sex, the killings, and the lack of anything positive, so out it went. Now, for us, the possibility didn't seem so far off anymore.
>
> At this time I was pregnant with my fourth child, and my husband definitely was not looking forward to my nursing another baby in front of daytime television. And the set was dying a slow death on its own. Though we couldn't quite

bring ourselves to toss it, when he suggested not getting a new one when this TV quit, or else getting rid of it when the baby was born, I was ready to say, "OK." That day came sooner than expected when I (yes, me) accidentally spilled my iced tea down into the back of the set, causing it to flash funny colors. *Poof!* It was gone.

Well, that TV ended up as parts for the little one-man appliance repair shop in town. We tried to sneak it to the car without the children noticing, but my eight-year-old came up right as we were going out the front door and asked, "What are you doing?" We told him we were giving it away, and he said, "Oh." There were no tears, no pleading, no fits. That was a surprise. Could it possibly be that it wasn't the children who were the TV-dependent ones, who now would have such a difficult time adjusting to life without it, who truly would be at a loss? On second thought, it's not surprising that I was the one who had the most trouble. Television was intertwined with more than just the superficial parts of my being. I learned how to read from *Sesame Street*, learned about racial issues from *All in the Family* and *The Cosby Show*. I learned about war from *M.A.S.H.* and justice from *Matlock*. Part of my life was lived by someone else on a set in Hollywood, and I accepted that as part of me, when really I was nothing but an advertising dollar. Knowing how connected my generation and I are to the world of television, I was surprised when I gave it up: it was much easier than I thought it would be. The giving it up was actually easy. The *decision* to do it was the hard part.

And now I can't say that life has been all that different. I forget that our going TV free must look very unusual to someone on the outside. But, from here, it appears quite the same. The immediate effects seem small, but I expect that, over a lifetime, they will be deep and dramatic, especially for the children. How very unknowingly wise I was to have done it now, while the children are young—for them, there is no loss.

There are times when I think that maybe we could have

kept it, that I could have developed the self-control to limit my viewing more severely, to be more choosy in my watching, to not give in to the mindless ease of turning the TV on because it's easier to do than the harder work of reading, talking, relating, living. But not once have I regretted this decision. And, aside from sometimes taking a little longer to get the news on the radio at the right time, I have not missed it a bit. Whether at friends' houses, in the waiting room at the doctor's office, in an airport, at McDonald's, or any of the countless other places television pops up—whenever I watch, I am reminded again and again of how little we are missing and what freedom we have gained by taking this choice seriously and enjoying its consequences.

Kate was only one of the hundreds of TV-free individuals who took a turn at the podium, eager to tell their stories. What they wrote was variously funny, serious, detailed, opinionated, and down-to-earth, but it was always loaded with passion for their choice to banish television from their lives. As they frequently remarked, one main reason they were presently TV free was that television had come to seem like "a lot of nothing." They spoke of TV as a time thief, a conversation stopper, and a black hole for the imagination. They were put off by the melodrama or the violence or the incessant commercials or by the narrow range of programming, despite the dozens of channels available. Although many of them acknowledged that here and there they might be missing a few worthwhile shows, they were also quick to point out that intelligent and perfectly reasonable replacement activities exist for even the very best historical program, news special, or nature documentary. Having turned the TV off, for whatever the original reason, they discovered that the two-dimensional screen just could not compete with multidimensional life—and so, in the end, these women and men simply lost the desire to spend any more time in front of the TV. As a result, relationships improved, children got their childhoods back, and life took a nice little turn into the "my choice" lane.

**Epilogue:
The One-Eyed Monster**

Author Barbara Kingsolver is one of the many Americans who are committed to a TV-free household. She is a member of the board of advisors of the Center for Screen-Time Awareness, and she has written one of the most eloquent, and amusing, testimonials to life without television that I have had the pleasure to encounter: "The One-Eyed Monster, and Why I Don't Let Him In." I would like to take this opportunity to quote some of what she has to say.

"Nobody ever gets killed at our house," begins a song by Charlie King, and it continues with a litany of other horrors— "no one gets shot at, run over, or stabbed, / nobody goes up in flames"—that you'd surely agree you wouldn't want to see in *your* house, either, until you realize he's discussing what routinely happens on the screen that most people happily host in their living rooms. Maybe you have one in yours, and maybe you don't, but I'm with Charlie. People very rarely get killed at our house, and I'm trying to keep it that way.

The subject isn't entirely closed, of course, because we are not Amish. We are what you'd call a regular American family, surrounded by regular America, and I believe in raising children who express themselves freely. This they do. The other night they raised the question once again of whether it might not be time for us to join the twenty-first century and every other upright-walking family we know of, at least in this neighborhood, and get cable TV.

"Why are you asking me?" I said, pretending to be dismayed. "Do I look like the dictator of this house?"

My efforts to stall weren't fooling anybody. I am not the dictator of this house, but I am the designated philosopher-king of its television-watching habits. That is to say, when my subjects become restless on the topic of TV, as they do from time to time, I sit down once again and explain to them in the kindest of tones why it is in their best interest to drop it.

But this time I'd been blindsided. Teenager and kinder-gartner were in league, with perhaps even the sympathies of my husband, though he was precluded from offering an opin-ion by his diplomatic ties. But the indentured serfs were fomenting a small rebellion.

"OK, look," I said to my serfs. "Watching TV takes *time*. When are you going to do it?"

They answered this without blinking: Evening. Morning. Prime time. Only when something good is on.

Which is just what I was afraid of. I explained that while I could understand there were probably some good things on TV that they were missing, they would have to miss out on *other* things in order to watch them, and when I looked around at what everybody was doing in our house, I couldn't really see what would give. I asked them, particularly my teenager (who likes to watch *Daria* and MTV at other people's houses, and whom I immediately sniffed out as our Robes-pierre here), to spend a few days paying careful attention to the hours of her life and exactly how she spent them. Kind of like keeping a calorie record, only with minutes. If she could come up with two expendable hours per day, I'd consider let-ting her spend them with the one-eyed monster.

She agreed to this, and at that moment I knew I'd already won. Here is what she does with her time: goes to school, does homework, practices the upright bass, talks with friends on the phone, eats dinner with the family, does more home-work, reads for fun, hangs out with friends at their houses or ours, works out, listens to music, jams on the electric bass, tries to form an all-girl band, maintains various pets, partici-pates in family outings, and gets exactly enough sleep. (In summertime the routine is different and the subject is moot, because then we live beyond the reach of cables, in a tiny house with no room for a TV and antique electricity that likely wouldn't support one anyway.) Her time card, in short, is full. Friends, exercise, music—not one minute of these would she give up, nor would I want her to. Even hanging out with friends—*especially* that—should not be sacrificed for solitary confinement with a talking box. If she wants to watch MTV at a friend's house, fine, that's *their* way of socializing—at our house her pals like to beat on my conga drums. And while she might have offered to trade in some hours of math homework, she knew better. Everything else she simply likes too much to cut out of her day.

So the discussion was shelved for the time being. I intend to keep a firm hand on at least this one aspect of my kingdom. To me, that ubiquitous cable looks an awful lot like the snake that batted its eyes at Eve.

Probably I shouldn't use such a morally loaded metaphor. I don't mean to equate my freedom from TV with freedom from sin, or to suggest that it confers on me any special virtue, though others generally interpret the discussion that way. If ever it comes up in conversation that my life is largely a TV void, people instantly get defensive about their own television-viewing habit and extol the value of the *few* things they like to watch (invariably citing something called the History Channel). But no defense is necessary, I promise; this is not about high-culture snobbery. If you knew me, you'd know there's almost nothing that is categorically beneath my dignity: I can get teary-eyed over a song about family reunions on the country radio station; I love to borrow my teenager's impractical shoes; on a dance floor I'm more at home with salsa and hip-hop than the tango; I have been known to do the Macarena. At a party more recent than I care to admit (I was definitely past forty), my friends voted me Most Likely to Dance on the Table. Before I dig this hole any deeper, why don't you just take my word for it? I'm not too high-minded for television; I really just don't like it. It's a taste I never got to acquire, having been raised by parents who made it painfully clear that life offered no bigger waste of time than watching the "boob tube" (one of the rare slang terms that've become more apt with the years). From there I proceeded to live an adult life with lots to do and very little cash, so that purposefully setting out to pay money for a time-wasting device just never crossed my mind. I made it to the childbearing phase without TV dependence, then looked around and thought, Well gee, why start *now*? Why get a pet python on the *day* you decide to raise fuzzy little gerbils?

The advantages of raising kids without commercial TV seem obvious, and yet I know plenty of parents who express dismay as their children demand sugar-frosted sugar for breakfast, then expensive name-brand clothing, then the right to dress up as hookers not for Halloween but for school. *Hello?* Anyone who feels powerless against the screaming voice of materialistic youth culture should remember that power comes out of those two little holes in the wall. The plug is detachable. Human young are not born with the knowledge that wearing somebody's name in huge letters on a T-shirt is a thrilling privilege for which they should pay eighty dollars. It takes years of careful instruction to arrive at that piece of logic.

I ask my kids, on principle, to live without wasteful and preposterous things (e.g., clothing that extorts from customers the right to wear labels on the outside), and it's a happier proposition to follow through if we don't have an extra blabbermouth in the room telling them every fourteen minutes about six brand-*new* wasteful, preposterous things they'll die without. It's fairly well documented that TV creates a net loss in contentment. The average household consumption of goods and services has doubled since 1957, when TV began to enter private homes, but according to a University of Chicago study, over all those years the fraction of Americans who describe themselves as "very happy" has remained steady, at about one third. The amount of money people believed they *needed* to buy happiness actually doubled between the mid-1980s and the mid-1990s, and the figure is still reaching for the sky. Think the kids would be unhappy without TV? I say

living outside the box

pull the plug, quick, before they get more miserable. My daughters are by no means immune to peer pressure, but the kindergartner couldn't pick Tommy Hilfiger out of a lineup, and the ninth grader dresses way cool on an impressively frugal clothing budget, and they both find a hundred things to do each day that are more fun than sitting in front of a box. They agree with me about TV, once they're forced to accept the theory that there are only twenty-four hours in a day.

■ ■ ■

As a habitual reader I find the pace of information delivery on television noticeably sluggish. There's a perfectly good reason for this: The script for a one-hour TV documentary is only about fifteen or twenty double-spaced pages in length, whereas most any competent reader can cover three to five times that much material in an hour. Devoted as our culture is to efficiency, convenience, and DSL Internet access, I'm surprised so many Americans are content to get their up-to-the-minute news delivered in such a slow, vacuum-packed format.

I did get a chance, recently, to watch CNN for a few minutes, and I was bedazzled by what I presume to be its post–September 11 format, in which the main story is at the top of the screen, "Coming Up Next" occupies the middle, and completely unrelated headlines run constantly across the bottom. Yikes. It looked to me like a TV trying very hard to be a newspaper, about as successfully as my five-year-old imitates her big sister's smooth teenage dance steps. Ten minutes of that visual three-ring circus gave me a headache; when I want *newspaper*, I'll read one.

It's true that being a reader rather than a viewer gives me a type of naïveté that amuses my friends. I'm in the dark, for instance, about what many public figures look like, at least in color rather than newsprint (for the longest time I thought Phil Donahue was *blond*), and in some cases I may not know quite how to pronounce their names. When people began talking about the dreadful anthrax attack on the congressional offices, I kept scratching my head and asking, "*Dashell?* There's a Senator *Dashell?*" It took me nearly a day to identify the man whose name my brain had been registering as something like "Dask-lee."

But I don't mind being somebody's fool. I don't think I'm missing too much. Of course, every two weeks or so someone will tell me about the latest should-be-required-viewing-for-the-human-race documentary that I've missed. No problem: I know how to send off for it, usually from Annenburg CPB. Then some winter evening I'll put the tape in the machine, and if I agree it's wonderful I will see it out. Often it turns out I've long since read an article that told me exactly the same things about Muslim women or Mongolian mummies unearthed or whatever-have-you, or a book that told me more. For bringing events quickly to the world, the imaginative reporter's pad and the still photographer's snap are far more streamlined instruments than bulky video cameras and production committees. But sometimes, I won't deny it, there is a video image that stops me cold and rearranges the furniture of my heart. An African mother's gesture of resignation, the throat-singing of a Tuva shepherd, a silent pan of the untouched horizon of a Central Asian steppe—these things can carry an economy of feeling in so many unspoken words that they're pure instruction for a wordy novelist. For exactly this reason I love to watch movies, domestic and especially foreign ones, and we see lots of them at home. We do own a VCR. My kids would point out to you that it's old and somewhat antiquated; I would point out that so am I, by some standards, but we both still work just fine.

I'm happy to use the machine; I just don't want a cable or a dish or an antenna. Having a sieve up there on the roof collecting wild beams from everywhere does seem poetic, but the image that strikes me as more realistic is that of a faucet into the house that runs about 5 percent clear water and 95 percent raw sewage. I know some people who stay on guard all the time and carefully manage this flow so their household gets a healthy intake; I know a lot more who don't. Call me a control freak, but I have this thing about my household appliances—blender, lawn mower, TV monitor—which is that I like to feel I am in charge of the machine, and not vice versa. I have gotten so accustomed to this balance of power with my VCR that I behave embarrassingly in front of real television. When I watch those stony-faced men (I swear one of them is named Stone) deliver the official news with their pursed mouths and woeful countenances, I feel compelled to mutter back at them, insolently, while my teenager puts her forearms over her face. (Now you know what I really am—more insolent than my own teenager.) "You're completely ignoring what *caused* this," I mumble at Ted-Peter-Dan, "and anyway who did your *hair*?"

Well, honestly, who do those guys think I am? Thirteen seconds of whatever incident produced the most alarming visuals today, and I'm supposed to believe that's all I really need to know? One overturned fuel tanker in Nebraska is more important to me than, say, global warming? Television news is driven by compelling visuals, not by the intrinsic importance of the story being cast. Complicated, nonphotogenic issues requiring any considerable background information (global warming, for example) get left out of the running every time.

Meanwhile, viewers are lured into assuming, at least subconsciously, that this "news" is a random sampling of everything that happened on planet earth that day, and so represents reality. One friend of mine argued (even though, as I say, I'm not trying to start a fight) that he felt a moral obligation to watch CNN so he could see all there was and sort out what was actually true—as if CNN were some huge window thrown wide on the whole world at once. Not true, not *remotely* true. The world, a much wider place than seventeen inches, includes songbird migration, emphysema, pollinating insects, the Krebs cycle, my neighbor who recycles knitting-factory scraps to make quilts, natural selection, the Loess Hills of Iowa, and a trillion other things outside the notice of CNN. Are they important? Everything on that list I just tossed off is life or death to somebody somewhere, half of them are life and death to you and me, and you may well agree that they're all more interesting that Monica Lewinsky. It's just a nasty, tiny subset of reality they're subsisting on there in TV land—the subset invested with some visual component likely to cause an adrenal reaction, ideally horror.

■ ■ ■

Still, there is this thing in us that wants to have a look, a curiosity that was quite useful to our ancestors on the savannah but is not so helpful now when it makes us rubberneck as we drive past the awful car crash. So the gods that gave us TV now bring us the awfulest car crash of the day and name it *The World Tonight*. This running real-time horror show provides a peculiarly unbalanced diet for the human psyche, tending to make us feel that we're living in the most dangerous time and place imaginable. When the eyes see a building explode, and then an airplane burning, and the ears hear, "Car bomb in Oklahoma City . . . far away from here . . . equipment failure . . . odds of this one in a million," the message stashed away by the brain goes something like, "Uh-oh, cars explode, buildings collapse, planes plunge to the ground— oh, *man*, better hunker down." As a person who either reads the news or hears it on the radio, I am a bit more of a stranger to this scary-world phenomenon, so I notice its impact on other people.

The day after all the world became a ghastly stage for the terrified high school students fleeing from murder by their classmates in Littleton, Colorado, it happened that I was to give an afternoon staff writing workshop at my sixth grader's school. When we assembled, I could see that the teachers

living outside the box

were jumpy and wanted to talk rather than write. Several confessed that they had experienced physical panic that morning at the prospect of coming to school. I sympathized with their anxiety, but since nobody ever gets shot in my house, I didn't share the visceral sense of doom that surely came from seeing a live-camera feed of bloody children just like ours racing from a school so very much like this one. I remarked that while the TV coverage might make us *feel* endangered, the real probability of our own kids getting shot at school today had been lower than the odds of their being bitten by a rattlesnake while waiting for the bus. And more to the point, the chance of such horrors happening here was hardly greater than it had been two days before, when we weren't remotely worried about it. (The TV coverage apparently did increase the likelihood of other school shootings, but only faintly.) It was such a small thing to offer—merely another angle on the truth—but I was amazed to see that it helped, as these thoughtful teachers breathed deeply, looked around at the quiet campus, and reclaimed the relative kindness of their lives. Anyone inclined toward chemical sedatives might first consider, seriously, turning off the TV.

6: regarding
   our children

A cartoon by Kirk Anderson depicts an American child at a world talent show. Children from other countries perform dance, sports, and drama. The spotlight shines on the American child, center stage, sitting cross-legged in front of a TV, holding a remote and switching channels.

In 1964, some 5 percent of American children were overweight. Today, the figure stands at more than 15 percent. In the past twenty-five years, the proportion of overweight children between the ages of six and eleven has doubled, while among adolescents the proportion has tripled.[1] A study conducted in 2003 by the Centers for Disease Control and Prevention found that 60 percent of children between the ages of nine and thirteen—"the most physically active period in most people's lives"—do not engage in sports other than at school.[2] In place of physical activity, kids are sitting in front of a TV screen, often snacking on candy, cookies, chips, and soda pop while they do—a pattern that prompted David Ruskin, executive director of Commercial Alert, to comment that "television is basically an obesity machine."[3]

Firm evidence of a connection between TV viewing and childhood obesity was provided in 1985 by researchers William Dietz and Stephen Gortmaker, whose findings correlated a 2 percent increase in the prevalence of obesity with each hour of television viewed.[4] Since then, the evidence for such a link has grown to be overwhelming. To make matters worse, the past few decades have seen an explosion of junk food commercials. Of the upwards of 40,000 TV ads that children see every year, nearly three-quarters—that is, 30,000 of them—are for candy (32%), cereal (31%), and fast food (9%).[5] Almost incredibly, one study documented 202 such ads during four hours of Saturday morning cartoons— approximately eight ads every ten minutes.[6] Research has also demonstrated that even two-year-olds not only recognize but will request particular food items merely on the basis of viewing a thirty-second commercial.[7] New, "educational" shows aimed at infants and toddlers have further contributed to the increase in childhood obesity. In the words of U.S. Surgeon General Dr. David Satcher, speaking at the start of TV-Turnoff Week in 2001: "We are raising the most overweight generation of youngsters in American history." Sad to say, Satcher is correct. As of 2004, roughly 20 percent of children between the ages of two and five and 30 percent of children aged six to nineteen were either overweight or at risk of being overweight. Nor is the problem likely to go away: a majority of obese adolescents—some 80 percent—will grow up to become obese adults.[8]

In recent years, attempts have been made to address the problem of childhood obesity through government funding in the areas of health and education. Millions of dollars have been spent trying to find the elusive "cure"—the magic formula that will get children off the couch. Between 2002 and 2005, for example, the Centers for Disease Control and Prevention mounted a multimillion-dollar nationwide media campaign called VERB, with the goal of persuading young adolescents to exercise. Actors dressed up as the popular cartoon character SpongeBob SquarePants appeared in cities across the country to promote physical activity—dancing, biking, running, jumping, and so forth. The campaign also paid large sums of money for slick commercials, aired during children's favorite TV shows, as well as ads in magazines targeted at "tweens" and their parents—ads that featured dozens of active, slender, happy-looking children doing verbs. The message was commendable. So what happened? The Bush administration decided the costs were too high and took a hatchet to the VERB campaign during one of its rounds of budget cuts.

Given that TV viewing is such a major contributor to the problem of obesity, perhaps spending tens of millions of dollars on television ads is

living outside the box

not the ideal way to encourage children to exercise. All the same, the program did appear to be having an effect: it had reportedly sparked a 30 percent increase in exercise among preteens. It is also hard to quarrel with the opinion of a panel convened by the Institute of Medicine, namely, that the fate of the VERB campaign casts doubt on the government's commitment to the prevention of obesity. Commenting on the demise of the campaign, Dr. Jeffrey Koplan, the head of the IOM panel and one of the CDCP's former directors, described childhood obesity as "a major health problem. It's of a different nature than acute, infectious threats, but it needs to be taken just as seriously." And yet initiatives aimed at preventing or reducing obesity are not only poorly organized at the national level—a few new bike paths in one town, better innercity access to recreational facilities in another—but chronically underfunded. "We are still not doing enough to prevent childhood obesity," Koplan warned, "and the problem is getting worse." Or, as a spokesperson for the Center for Science in the Public Interest put it, "What the country is doing is like putting a Band-Aid on a brain tumor."[9] Our society prides itself on the attention it lavishes on its children. Why, then, have we been so slow to react to what is clearly a looming health crisis among our youth? One can only wonder whether part of the explanation could be that watching television is such a well-loved activity among parents as well as their children.

In 2005, California passed legislation prohibiting the sale of soda pop and fast food items in its public schools, a bill that public health officials hailed as marking "the most impressive gains in school nutrition since school lunch was introduced after World War II."[10] Schools elsewhere have likewise begun to tackle the issue of obesity by taking soda pop and junk food out of their vending machines. These are admirable steps, and one can only hope that the spark will start a fire with parents at home. But better nutrition is only the beginning. Unfortunately, too many schools pay only lip service to the importance of physical activity in the curriculum. Owing in part to budgetary constraints, more and more schools are cutting back on the length of recess periods or the number of required physical education classes—measures that not only encourage inactivity in our youth but often narrow the range of sports activities in which they have an opportunity to participate. Government grants are available to aid schools in implementing innovative physical education programs intended to instill lifetime habits that emphasize walking and movement and to foster an appreciation of sports. The onus is on overworked teachers and school administrators, however, to apply for such grants. Each active minute at school helps, of course. *But the average American child, just like his or her parents, still spends several hours each day doing nothing but staring at a screen.*

Children are, moreover, being lured to the TV at ever younger ages. Since its debut in 1997, BBC television's *Teletubbies*, the first TV show aimed at babies and toddlers, has drawn tiny tots to the screen in droves. The program is shown in this country on PBS stations, and parents rave about its mesmerizing power and the calming effect it has on their little ones, who can be seen to sit motionless and quiet before the screen—very unusual behavior for young children during their waking hours. In 2004, Anne Woods, the creator of *Teletubbies*, premiered a new show called *Boohbah*, geared to children aged from three to six and intended to encourage them to exercise. After a warm-up dance, each installment features a storytelling sequence, followed by the Boohbah dance. The American version of *Boohbah* then adds another dance, this one performed by real children and designed to be simple enough to allow the at-home audience to join in. Once again, the idea is commendable. At the same time, the claims of TV producers to have developed shows that actually generate an enthusiasm for exercise must be approached with a certain skepticism. Those employed in the TV industry are understandably very eager to persuade parents that watching television can actually be part of the *cure* for childhood obesity, rather than part of the cause—an argument that "has about as much merit as the antismoking ads run by tobacco companies."[11] *So why won't parents simply turn off the TV for the sake of their toddlers?*

The Cartoon Network, with its "Tickle U" block of programming, also aims at capturing the preschool audience for a couple of hours every morning. The network claims that their programs help develop children's sense of humor and that evidence exists to support this claim. But, as a recent editorial in *Chicago Parent* pointed out, the evidence in question consists of "general research about how children develop a sense of humor, not research that shows television viewing helps children develop a sense of humor. There is no research on that."[12] The Campaign for a Commercial-Free Childhood (among others) has encouraged parents to boycott the Tickle U programming. "Children don't need TV to develop a sense of humor," argues Diane Levin, author of *Remote Control Childhood? Combating the Hazards of Media Culture*. "It comes from play and their natural interactions with the world around them. This is a classic case of marketers trying to create a need where none exists and to dupe parents into thinking that watching more TV is good for their children."[13] Indeed, parents would do well to heed a warning from the American Academy of Pediatrics: "Although certain television programs may be promoted to this age group, research on early brain development shows that babies and toddlers have a critical need for direct interactions with parents and other significant caregivers (e.g., child care providers) for healthy brain growth and the development of appropriate social, emotional, and cognitive skills."[14]

Although research into TV viewing and children's cognitive development is swiftly accumulating, the relationship between the two is far from completely understood. The average TV screen is not very large, which makes visual details hard to take in and appreciate. To hold the attention of viewers, television programs (and, above all, commercials) often rely instead on a succession of quick cuts, so that the image before the viewer is constantly changing. Studies of the brain's reaction to a series of visual stimuli have shown that increasing the frequency with which images change can actually improve memory recognition. But only to a point. Research has also shown that if visual stimuli change too frequently—when the number of cuts exceeds about ten in two minutes—memory recognition ceases to improve. An extremely rapid style of editing, of the sort pioneered by music videos and subsequently borrowed by commercials, ultimately results in sensory overload—the inability to retain any message, and hence to learn.[15]

A similar trend has been visible in children's programming. For the more than three decades the show was on the air, Mister Rogers slowly and methodically told children what he was going to say, said it, and then reminded them of what he had said, all in the course of taking off his jacket and putting on his cardigan and slippers. The slow pace of the show drove some parents crazy, but children didn't seem to mind, and the repetition no doubt helped them absorb the message. Then came the innovative *Sesame Street*, which inaugurated a style characterized by quick changes of setting and theme—a style that has proved very popular. Critics of the fast-paced approach to children's programming argue, however, that over the years such programs actually shorten a child's attention span and inhibit his or her reading ability. "Reading demands sustained voluntary attention from a mind that can hold a train of thought long enough to reflect on it," writes educational psychologist Jane Healy, "not one accustomed to having its attention jerked around every few seconds."[16]

Research suggests that critics such as Healy may very well be correct. For instance, a study based on a sample of 2,623 one- and three-year-olds, the results of which appeared in the April 2004 issue of *Pediatrics*, found that each additional hour of daily television viewing in very young children is associated with a statistically significant increase in their risk of suffering attention-deficit problems.[17] Those who deal with children on a daily basis have reached much the same conclusion. As Frank Vespe, former director of the TV-Turnoff Network (now the Center for Screen-Time Awareness), commented to me in a telephone interview, "For many years, teachers and doctors have told us that, in their experience, many of the children who have the most difficulty focusing and paying attention are also the heaviest TV watchers." One highly controversial piece of research, carried out by three economists at Cornell's Johnson Graduate School of Management, has even attempted to link heavy TV viewing in very young children with the development of autism.[18]

In the meanwhile, physical and verbal aggression has been on the rise for years in schools, possibly because, in addition to their exposure to onscreen violence and the inappropriate messages they receive from media of all kinds, children lack adequate outlets for their physical energy. "Power Ranger" antics in the playground, classmates kick-boxing each other, bomb scares, threatening notes, children toting guns: these are very scary incidents, and far from uncommon in schools today. Violent television programming and video games have been repeatedly

living outside the box

linked to an increase in aggressive behavior among youth. To cite just one of innumerable examples, a study by Frederick J. Zimmerman and colleagues found that the greater the amount of television a child watches at the age of four, the greater the chances that the child will engage in bullying of classmates once he or she is in grade school. "Violence on TV isn't just *The Sopranos*," Zimmerman noted. "Kids' TV often has a particularly bad kind of violence—the humorous kind."[19] In a call for "media education," the American Academy of Pediatrics takes as conclusively established that "significant exposure to media violence increases the risk of aggressive behavior in certain children and adolescents, desensitizes them to violence, and makes them believe that the world is a 'meaner and scarier' place than it is."[20]

Because the principal task of very young children is learning, their minds are naturally more malleable and impressionable than those of adults. Children are thus far more apt to internalize what they observe—to accept it as reliable information and use it in shaping long-term values. As a result, exposure to violence at an early age tends to have enduring consequences. A study of both the short- and long-term effects of exposure to media violence led researchers to conclude: "Parents need to be as concerned about the beliefs and attitudes that are being conveyed in violent shows as they are about their child mimicking the behaviors shown. The changes in how the child perceives the world from viewing violence and the beliefs about aggression that the child acquires from viewing violence are likely to influence the child's behavior in the long term."[21]

It is common knowledge that children are tempted to practice what they see, without necessarily giving much thought to, or even having a clear understanding of, the outcome of brutal actions. Mike Smajda, principal of Lemmer Elementary School in Escanaba, Michigan, was horrified when he learned that one of his first-grade pupils had seen the film *The Texas Chainsaw Massacre*. The same young boy was subsequently involved in an incident in which a fellow student was kicked until her head was bloodied. "He felt it was part of the game," Smajda commented. This frightening incident, which occurred in 2004, served to reinforce Smajda's commitment to an innovative program called Student

Media Awareness to Reduce Television (SMART), developed by researchers at Stanford University. Their approach was to cut out all violent programming on screens of any sort—TV, video games, and other electronic forms of entertainment—for ten days and after that to limit a child's exposure to onscreen violence to seven hours a week. Observers charted the number of aggressive playground incidents—shoving, hitting, name-calling—at eight elementary schools before and after students took part in the SMART program. Even though some of the children complained that turning off their screens was "boring" and "miserable," on average their involvement in acts of aggression declined by 52 percent. Moreover, their test scores improved.[22]

In 2000, Thomas Robinson, of Stanford University's School of Medicine, carried out several studies with a sample of 900 schoolchildren who limited their TV viewing to six hours each week. After six weeks, the incidence of verbal and physical aggression among these children had decreased by 25 percent.[23] In another study, which involved sixteen preschools in Cooperstown, New York, researchers implemented a series of seven 20-minute sessions designed to reduce TV viewing. Children compiled lists of activities that could serve as alternatives to watching television and received a special sticker each day they survived without TV. By the end of the seven sessions, the children who had participated had reduced their viewing time by close to 25 percent, and the proportion of children who watched TV or videos for more than two hours daily had dropped from 33 percent to only 18 percent.[24] In short, children's TV habits *can* be changed, and the change can make a substantial difference to their outlook and behavior.

An Uncontrolled Experiment   Over the years, largely at the urging of parents and other concerned groups, technology has tackled the problem of how to limit what children see on TV. The V-chip allows parents to block certain channels or programs; TiVo's Kid-Zone likewise enables parents to select the programs their children will watch. In addition, schools and colleges have undertaken campaigns for media literacy that seek to educate children (and adults) about the way advertising works, to foster critical thinking skills, and to encourage a thoughtful approach to media consumption. As we have seen, assorted attempts have also been made to attract children to a less sedentary lifestyle. The fact remains, however, that American children continue to watch prodigious amounts of TV—good, bad, and indifferent. Although we profess to be worried about the effects of television on young and innocent minds, how well do we actually understand the situation? Do we really know what all those hours in front of the TV are doing to our children?

Marie Winn, author of *The Plug-In Drug*, is disappointed with the quality of attention that has been paid to certain fundamental issues regarding children and television. She asks: (1) What is the effect on the developing human organism when a significant portion of each day is devoted to watching instead of active play? (2) What impact does television have on language development? (3) Is a child's perception of reality skewed in any way by watching television? (4) Does the availability of TV influence the way parents raise their children? (5) How does watching TV for several hours each day affect a child's ability to form human relationships?[25] Despite an immense amount of research, these and other questions remain to be adequately explored. In the estimation of pediatrician Donald Shifrin, "We are conducting an ongoing, uncontrolled experiment on this generation in terms of media exposure and potential future behavioral and physical consequences, and it seems unopposed by the media industry and most parents."[26]

The major media corporations may indeed be partly responsible for the apparent resistance to studying the situation in greater depth. These corporations wield far too much power over the politicians who direct the government agencies that in turn fund social and scientific research. However, also responsible, certainly, is the continued widespread denial that television really is such a big problem. As Winn notes, "The fact that these questions are rarely raised, that the meaning of the experience itself is rarely considered, signals the distorted view American parents take of television's impact on their children and families."[27]

If we, as parents, are to some extent complicit in the problem, reasons are not hard to find. For one thing, television is remarkably convenient: it occupies children, thereby allowing parents to do other things. In a landmark study carried out by the Kaiser Family Foundation—*Zero to Six: Elec-*

tronic Media in the Lives of Infants, Toddlers, and Preschoolers (2003)—nearly half (45 percent) of parents of children aged six and under said that when they have something important to do, it is quite likely that they will use TV as a babysitter.[28] Similarly, parents who participated in a subsequent KFF study, *The Media Family*, frequently called attention to how very busy they are and argued that they had little choice but to rely on television to keep their kids amused while they themselves are doing chores. Parents also spoke about their need for time to themselves, which many of them engineered by first setting their kids up in front of a TV show or a DVD. Some worried about allowing their children to play outdoors without supervision or about what their children might get up to if they weren't safely positioned in front of the TV. As one mother commented, "If the TV isn't on, he's putting the 'Orange Glo' all over my daughter's bedspread. That makes more work for me."[29] These are all valid concerns. The question is whether using television as a babysitter is as harmless a practice as parents tend to assume. As one mother thoughtfully conceded, allowing her children to watch television "makes my life easier now, but in the long run, when they're older and starting to run into all these problems, I think I'll wish I wouldn't have let them do it when they were five."[30]

The problem is compounded by the fact that a great many parents are themselves avid TV viewers. Roughly two-thirds of the children in the *Zero to Six* study lived in homes where the television was on at least half the time, even when no one was watching it, and over a third in homes where the TV was "always" on or on "most of the time."[31] The authors of *The Media Family* concluded that "parents' beliefs about media—and their own media habits—are strongly related to how much time their children spend with media, the patterns of their children's use, and the types of content their children are exposed to." As the authors of the study discovered, "parents who are big TV fans and hate the interruptions from their little ones are more likely to get a TV for their children's bedroom"—something that has the added advantage (as some 55 percent of these parents pointed out) of reducing competition for the set and thus allowing every family member to watch his or her favorite programs.[32] Understandably, parents are not eager to believe that something they themselves engage in and enjoy, or simply feel compelled to rely on,

living outside the box

could actually retard their children's brain development or hinder their acquisition of linguistic, motor, and social skills or even undermine their reality testing. In the words of Jane Healy, "Parents do not want to hear that the amount of TV their children watch has caused them problems in school. It's easier to say, 'He has a brain disorder.'"[33]

Parents, especially parents who are themselves heavy TV viewers, also seem reluctant to lay down basic rules governing how much television their children are allowed to watch, and when. In another Kaiser Family Foundation report, *Generation M: Media in the Lives of 8- to 18-Year-olds* (2005), over half the children surveyed—53 percent—reported that their parents had no rules whatsoever regarding TV viewing. Another 23 percent said that such rules *did* exist but were never or not always enforced. In households in which parents did have established rules governing TV, however, and expected children to abide by these rules, children's daily media exposure dropped by close to two hours (1 hour, 50 minutes).[34] Needless to say, parents would prefer to avoid the arguments that are bound to ensue when efforts are made to control their children's TV viewing. But does allowing children unrestricted access to TV constitute a reasonable alternative?

It is now well established that, as children's TV viewing increases, their academic performance deteriorates. More than one to two hours a day of television has been consistently linked to a diminished interest in school activities and poorer grades, especially in reading.[35] And yet our children continue to spend considerably more time watching television than they do in school.[36] Granted, in recent years the number of hours that children devote to television appears to have leveled off—but evidently this is because television has to some extent been supplanted by other forms of electronic entertainment. The authors of *Generation M* discovered that between 1999 and 2004 children's TV viewing had held steady, averaging just over three hours a day. In the space of those five years, however, the total amount of media content to which children were exposed daily had increased by more than an hour, going from 7 hours and 29 minutes to 8 hours and 33 minutes, with most of the increase coming from video games (up by 23 minutes) and computer use not related to schoolwork (up by 35 minutes). By way of contrast, children reported spending only 50 minutes a day on homework, 43 minutes reading, and 32 minutes on chores.[37] Again, television was a looming presence in a great many households: 63 percent of these children reported that the TV was "usually" on during meals, and just over half said it was on "most" or "all" of the time.[38] The research also indicated that nearly 7 out of 10 of these children (68 percent) had a television set in their bedroom, on top of which 54 percent also had a VCR or DVD player, and 49 percent a video game player. Not surprisingly, children equipped with their own private TV watched more television than did other children—on the average, an additional hour and a half each day.[39] Statistics such as these raise issues that should be of serious social concern. Yet television continues as the trusted companion of millions of children.

The situation is complicated by the fact that children are spending more time "media multitasking"—engaging with two or more media at once. As a result, a single hour of media use can translate into considerably more than an hour of exposure to media content. The children surveyed in the *Generation M* study racked up that daily total of 8 hours and 33 minutes' worth of media exposure in only 6 hours and 21 minutes of actual media use. Over a period of five years, the amount of time children spent media multitasking had increased by 10 percent, going from 16 percent of total media time to 26 percent.[40] Between a quarter and a third reported using another medium "most of the time" while they were watching TV (24%), reading (28%), listening to music (33%), or using a computer (33%).[41] Drew Altman, president and CEO of the Kaiser Family Foundation, summed it up: "Multitasking is a growing phenomenon in media use, and we don't know whether it's good or bad or both."[42]

Common sense tells us that when we try to focus on two things at once, we don't focus on either of them as well as we might. But what happens to us, not only cognitively but psychologically, as we spend ever more time with our attention divided? Do we experience greater stress as a result of our efforts to process input from two or more sources simultaneously? Or do we simply become accustomed to concentrating less well—and, if so, what are the consequences of this? It may be that habitual multitasking conditions the brain to an overexcited state, making it difficult for us to slow down and concentrate on a single task when we need to. As David E. Meyer, director of the Brain, Cognition, and Action

living outside the box

Laboratory at the University of Michigan, explains: "People lose the skill and the will to maintain concentration, and they get mental antsyness."[43] In addition, functional MRI studies have demonstrated that the human brain has, in fact, only a very limited ability to perform two tasks simultaneously. Such a feat is possible only when one (or both) of the tasks is so simple and so familiar as to be all but automatic. We may think that we are writing an email, talking on the phone, and downloading a new software program all at the same time, but what we are really doing is toggling rapidly among tasks. Under such circumstances, the likelihood of error increases substantially. Moreover, it actually takes *longer* to complete the tasks than it would if they were performed in sequence.[44]

Parents naturally tend to believe that they are doing the right and generous thing by providing their children with cell phones, computers, sound systems, televisions, DVD players, and so on right there in their bedrooms. They want their children to be happy, to fit in, and to excel. But to excel in what? Their good intentions notwithstanding, parents fail to recognize that their materially privileged children are being encouraged to spend the bulk of their free time isolated in their rooms, deprived of face-to-face interaction—essentially being raised by machines. But children (young children, especially) need human contact, not just sound and pictures on a two-dimensional screen. A report released in October 2004 by the Alliance for Childhood found that "scant evidence" exists of "long-term benefits of immersing preschool- and school-age children in electronic technologies."[45] In the opinion of some researchers, particularly in the case of very young children, such practices may even be harmful. "The computer software that's being rushed into market is training kids to be attention deficit disordered," argues Jane Healy. "It's training them to be impulsive, to have meager finger control because they're just using a small part of their motor system. These are the hallmarks of attention deficit disorder."[46]

This is not to suggest that electronic media are inherently an evil thing. Nor would I propose that we turn our backs on technological advances—which are, in any event, here to stay. But I would like to join others in issuing a plea for balance. As psychiatrist Edward Hallowell astutely observes: "The problem is what you are *not* doing if the electronic moment grows too large. You are not having family dinner, you are not having a conversation, you are not debating whether to go out with a boy who wants to have sex on the first date, you are not going on a family ski trip or taking time just to veg. It's not so much that the video game is going to rot your brain; it's what you are not doing that's going to rot your life."[47] The American Academy of Pediatrics has repeatedly advised parents to keep televisions out of children's rooms, not to allow children under the age of two to watch TV, and after that to limit children to a maximum of two hours of "quality programming" per day. Parents are also urged to "encourage more interactive activities that will promote proper brain development, such as talking, playing, singing, and reading together."[48] That said, pediatricians may need to work harder to disseminate their academy's recommendations: in one recent study, only 15 percent of parents reported that their pediatrician had ever raised the subject of their children's media use.[49]

What Our Children Are Not Doing

In 1990, the American Family Research Council reported that the average American parent spent 38.5 minutes in meaningful conversation with his or her children each week. That's less than six minutes a day.[50] Given that our TV viewing has spiraled steadily upward since then, chances are the situation today is no better. Such a statistic suggests that, for most children in America, adults are not terribly accessible. They are busy, or tired, or preoccupied. Their influence is fragile, even negligible, compared to that of the television. For children raised without television, however, circumstances are different. The parents who participated in my survey of TV-free families reported spending an average of 55 minutes *per day* in meaningful conversation with their children. That's 385 minutes a week—ten times the average reported back in 1990 for parents in TV-dominated households. Granted, my respondents may have been overly generous in their estimates. But even if we adjust the figure downward by as much as 20 percent, that's still 44 minutes a day, which is considerably better than six minutes. If "We got our time back" was probably the comment I most often heard

living outside the box

from TV-free parents, "We got our kids back" was certainly a close second. Or, to put it the other way around, TV-free kids got their parents back.

One participant in the study, Casey, recalled that when she was growing up, she felt that she had to compete with the television for the attention of her parents and sister. "We lived in a rural area, and I very much resented the time my sister spent glued to the TV. I have vivid recollections of wishing we would do things together as a family, like my friend Patti's family did, but there were only a few times that happened. The most memorable time was when we lived at a mountain cabin for six weeks, and we had no outside communication except for a radio. We played together as a family for the first time I could remember. When we came back to civilization, I felt a sense of being abandoned, as we were back to evenings of total TV. I often would play games alone while my mother, father, and sister sat like zombies." A remarkable number of the TV-free adults who took part in my survey complained of having been "forced" to watch TV when they were children because it was the family's one and only form of recreation and thus the only candidate for a shared activity.

One thing the average TV-viewing child tends to miss out on, then, is family interaction. But having a real conversation, along with the bonds this creates, is merely one of an endless number of opportunities for good leisure that are lost to television. Reading, creative pursuits, sports and other outdoor activities, hobbies and crafts of all kinds, doing puzzles and playing games that require several participants, active and imaginative play with friends—the list could go on indefinitely, for the simple reason that life holds infinite possibilities. To take one example: after purchasing land out in the countryside, Kim and her husband ran into problems hooking up to electricity when they began building a house on the property. In the end, they chose to power their new home by means of solar panels, and so they decided not to bother with television. "Since we've been living off the grid," Kim wrote, "my children, ages five, eight, and eleven, have been without question happier and healthier. They have never—not once—complained of being bored without TV. In their newly discovered time, they have learned new skills—knitting, drawing, dance. Watching my children thrive without TV has strengthened my resolve never to let it into my home again." During their first several weeks without TV, she reported, her children invented their own theatre, devising skits and performing for themselves. Her eleven-year-old daughter also found that she enjoys writing poetry.

My own children, Adam and Sydney, who were twelve and eight when my TV-free survey was conducted, offered a wealth of good examples of what can happen in the hours that a child might otherwise spend sitting in front of the TV. On one quite typical day, after the school bus dropped them off, they walked up the road, taking a route through the woods to look for bugs and snakes, which extended what would normally be an eight-minute walk to half an hour. When they got home, Sydney ate a snack consisting of some dill pickles and slices of cheese plus a few Oreos. Then she played with a Lego set and with dolls for about an hour and read a story from her new magazine, *Pockets*. After that she practiced the piano, took her dog outside to play, and worked in a coloring book. About three-quarters of an hour before dinner, she got out all her horse books and began writing a report for school. Adam also fixed himself a snack—chips and salsa, followed by some peanut butter, dill pickles, and cheese—which he ate while reading the comics. He did some homework, practiced his guitar, and drew for a while in a sketchbook. Then he went to help a neighbor with a chore and took his soccer ball outside for an hour before dinner. Some of their afternoons would include time spent with friends, an after-school sports practice or music lesson, or greater amounts of homework. But the point is that they had no trouble entertaining themselves for hours at a time. They walked and ran, talked, solved problems, created, fantasized, read, played outside, and relaxed. These activities took up roughly the same amount of time that most American children spend sitting in front of the television.

For the Sake of Our Children

An online survey conducted in April 2004 by *Scholastic News*, which drew about 15,000 responses, asked children whether they could live without television. Two-thirds of them said no.[51] Small wonder, perhaps, when the vast bulk of a typical schoolchild's

living outside the box

recreation time is spent watching TV. But when two out of three children regard television as indispensable to life, something is wrong. It is abundantly evident that too many hours in front of the TV contribute substantially to many of the ills besetting our children. Yet it is still seldom suggested that we simply *turn off the television*—the easiest, most obvious, and least expensive means of addressing the problem. Rather remarkably, this wonderfully simple idea continues to be viewed as ludicrous or impossible or both. All the same, the option does exist. The prevailing pattern *could* be changed, provided parents are willing to intervene.

Consider the experience of Dale and Laura, two of the TV-free parents who participated in my survey. Prior to their decision to get rid of the television, their viewing habits were well within line of the country's four-plus-hours-a-day average. In addition, their two preschoolers were exposed to every cartoon show imaginable at their daycare center, sometimes for as much as four or five hours each day. The children's behavior was already atrocious and getting worse. They knew every commercial, every jingle, every slogan, as well as all the right products to beg for. Finally, in a desperate attempt to do something about the situation, Dale and Laura decided to try going TV free. At first, Laura reported, their children required considerably more attention and "cleaning up after." But it wasn't long before they began to play on their own and be less demanding of their parents' time. Laura also spoke with the daycare director concerning the excessive amount of TV that the children were watching—and rightly so. A great many daycare services, probably somewhere around 70 percent, employ television or videos as a babysitter for a portion of the day.[52] If parents wish to control their children's exposure to such media, they need to speak up.

Linda and Rob simply did not want their daughter to grow up with television. "Young children have no filtering system for their environment," Linda pointed out. "They literally accept every image and impression they are exposed to as reality. What is on TV? Violence as an acceptable way to problem-solve, and the promotion of indiscriminate sexual behavior with no consequences. Additionally, TV commercials promote mass-market consumerism with its many inherent problems. We believe these are inappropriate values to put in front of young children." Her point about children's lack of critical filters is well taken. One of the survey respondents, Ellen, mentioned that when her young sons visit their grandparents and see news broadcasts, they come home and report that their grandparents live in a frightening neighborhood, even though her own family actually lives in a much larger city than do her parents. Speaking of the TV-free approach that she and her husband have adopted with their children, Ellen commented: "Our decisions are not based on a desire to shield the boys from the world. I believe they have to learn to get along in the world, but I also think children are growing up too quickly and that parents have to work at preserving childhood."

Darin and Tricia turned off the TV for the sake of their two-year-old son. Darin summed up their reasons clearly and succinctly. "Our belief is based upon two components," he wrote. "One: content, which perverts human perceptions of reality in so many ways. And the shows are sexist, racist, violent, and generally go against everything we're attempting to instill in our son. Two: the medium itself, which we believe affects a developing child's senses physiologically, mostly by keeping them from active learning, searching, discovering, and playing. We just chose not to subject our son to all that stuff." Their viewpoint was echoed by the observations of another mother, Meg, who commented, "In retrospect, we realize that not having the constant onslaught of popular culture in our house has made raising our children easier. They have long attention spans, excellent vocabularies, good problem-solving skills and social skills, empathy for those less fortunate than they are, and they've inherited our own values—not consumer oriented, pop-culture values and the accompanying narcissism. There is so much that one can do other than watch TV!"

Difficult as it might be to combat SpongeBob, sometimes children must be forced to find alternatives to television, must be challenged to turn it off for a week or a month or a year. "The difference between children who can picture a story or scene in their mind's eye and those who were raised in front of a TV screen are obvious and very profound," wrote Sue, a TV-free mother who is also a kindergarten teacher. "This difference is evident in their play, their artwork, their writing, the foods packed in their lunchboxes, their show-and-tell, and their conversation. TV perme-

living outside the box

ates every facet of their being. I think children raised with screens have never experienced what it's like to dream, create, and imagine inside their own heads—independent of an externally supplied (usually corporate) vision." Any parent knows that children are inventive creatures, endowed with a natural love of play and the ability to find solutions to boredom. At the same time, they don't always know what is best for them. They lack experience of the world, and thus it is up to parents to provide guidance and oversight. And this, in turn, requires not only that parents take time to educate themselves but that they be willing to make changes in their own behavior, if necessary, for the sake of their children.

7: thirty days
without television

*I really didn't like turning off the TV
except I noticed my grades went up and
I was in a good mood all week.*

—Drew Henson,
second-grader,
after participating in
National TV-Turnoff Week

Daniel, a sixth-grader at Cheney Middle School, never thought he could enjoy playing with his three sisters. But a month without television changed his mind. Riding his bike and other outdoor activities, along with having fun with his siblings, were, he informed me, "actually better than watching TV." Perhaps Daniel would eventually have stumbled on this discovery on his own. Chances are, though, he needed some outside prompting.

In the spring of 2003, by way of an experiment, I organized a pilot study in three local public schools. Called "30 Days Live," the study challenged children to go for a month without spending time in front of screens of any sort—televisions or computers. The experiment was so successful and received such wholehearted support from teachers that two years later it was repeated. A total of 130 fourth-, fifth-, and sixth-graders, from six different classrooms, participated in the two studies, 56 in 2003 and 74 in 2005. These children had been accustomed to anywhere from two to four hours of television a day before "30 Days Live" got underway.

At the end of each study, the students, their teachers, and their parents were asked to comment on the experience. By all accounts, the children had thrived. Even though almost half of them had predicted they would fail, just over three-quarters made it through the entire month.[1] During their time away from TV and computer screens, they had been more physically active and had engaged in conversation more often and for longer periods of time. They had consumed less junk food and gotten more sleep, and they had devoted considerably more time to pets. Overall, their mood had improved, and so had their grades. Six-month follow-ups revealed that nearly 80 percent of the children were watching less TV than they had before taking part in "30 Days Live." When the children were asked whether they would like to repeat the experiment, 97 percent said "Yes." Almost as many—93 percent—felt that kids all across the country would benefit from turning off their TVs and computer screens for thirty days.

| "30 Days Live": An Overview | Several days before the start of the thirty-day period, the students were given a small, spiral-bound journal. |

They were asked to record their before- and after-school activities and what they consumed by way of snacks—information that would allow me to form a baseline picture of their habits, with which their subsequent reports could then be contrasted. The journals were inscribed with quotations and statistics ("Did you know that the average kid spends 900 hours a year in school and 1,023 hours watching TV?"), gathered mostly from the Web site of the Center for Screen-Time Awareness, that were intended to help with motivation. The students were also given space to describe, in writing or drawing, the difficulties they were encountering as well as their joys and discoveries. At the start of each journal was a brief quiz, to be completed at the outset of the study, that was designed to assess the students' attitudes and their readiness to change; at the end was a short closing questionnaire. Each child's weight and Body Mass Index (BMI)—a measure of the relative amount of body fat—was recorded at the start and finish of the study. With the aid of pedometers, I also attempted to measure the number of steps each student took within a 48-hour period. Unfortunately, though, the pedometers proved to be difficult to regulate, and the data gathered had to be discarded. By the end

living outside the box

of the thirty days, however, nearly 60 percent of the participants had lost weight. For children who initially weighed between 90 and 100 pounds the average loss was 1.5 pounds; for those weighing over 100 pounds it was 2.9 pounds.

While the study was underway, the students were asked to rank, on a scale of one to five, how they felt each day, from "very bored" to "fabulous." At the end of the very first day, and then again at the end of the first, second, third, and fourth weeks, the students were interviewed in small groups, and their answers recorded. They were asked, for example: "What were your top three replacements for television during the past week?" "How much support are you getting at home, from your parents and your siblings?" and "What tips can you share that might help others stay away from TV for a whole month?" They also received handouts containing fun ideas for possible screen-free activities.

At the end of each week, the students who had survived were given a small prize. The prizes were purposely kept minor (their total cost was less than eight dollars a person) in accordance with an underlying hypothesis, namely, that intrinsic motivation would prove to outweigh the promise of extrinsic rewards. I had a feeling that if the children could get over the hump of the first week, during which they would begin to discover new ways of having fun, the fun itself would become their primary motivation. Those who made it through the first week received something "writable": a silly pen, covered with a fish-shaped piece of foam. Two-week survivors were treated to something "eatable": a pizza party. Those who lasted three weeks received something "playable": a small game box containing pickup sticks, dominoes, and playing cards. Those who made it through the entire thirty days received something "wearable": a red, white, and blue ribbon medallion with the "30 Days Live" logo on it.

At the close of the study, all the children—whether they had lasted one day or all thirty—were asked to complete the wrap-up survey, which consisted of thirteen questions listed at the end of the journal. Among the questions were:

- What was the most difficult day of the week and time of day for you to remain TV free?

- Would you say that any of the following improved over the time you were off TV: health, fitness, relationships, nutrition, attitude and mood, or sleeping habits? Any others?
- Were there any negative aspects of your experience?
- How do you now plan to deal with TV in your life?

Reports from the Children

The question concerning the most difficult day of the week and time of day produced answers that were fairly evenly dispersed across the range of possibilities. Monday through Sunday each received about the same number of votes for the most difficult day, and roughly as many children said they had the hardest time in the morning, before school, as said the hardest time was after school. Questions about how their feelings and their habits had changed over the thirty days generally elicited extremely positive responses, as well as generating plenty of group discussion. When asked what they had disliked or found difficult about the experience, several children lamented missing out on the latest episode of a favorite show or said they found it hard to give up playing Game Boy or Nintendo. Even so, most of them agreed that getting through the first week had been easier than they'd thought it would be.

The children were also asked to describe what they had done instead of watching TV or sitting in front of the computer. Evidently, they had found plenty to do. The top replacement activities were outdoor play, conversation with friends or family, reading, drawing, and games. Some reported that they'd reorganized their bedrooms, or discovered long-lost toys, or tried out a new hobby. Included in play activities was time spent with pets, who clearly enjoyed a lot more attention during the thirty days. It was apparent that the children sometimes borrowed ideas about possible activities from one another, often in the course of classroom discussions or the small-group interviews. For example, in reply to a question about what they'd chosen to do on their first TV-free day, one boy said, "I played with my scooter." Three others exchanged looks, and whispers were heard: "Hey! I have a scooter, too!" Soon, pieces of recreational equipment that had long been gathering dust were being brought out and used.

A little over half of the children (53 percent) predicted they would succeed in making it through the entire thirty days, and four out of five of them (81 percent) turned out to be correct. The others predicted they would fail—and yet a majority of the naysayers (72 percent) actually ended up succeeding. In other words, those who predicted success were very likely to make it, and those who predicted failure were still quite likely to make it.[2] Of course, not all of the children managed to last the duration. "I tried the first night," said fourth-grader Mitchell, "but then it seemed like I couldn't live without TV. All my favorite shows, especially *Everybody Loves Raymond*, were on, and I just couldn't hold it!" Bryan lasted a little longer—three days—before the pull of *The Simpsons* and *Futurama* proved irresistible. By the halfway point, 21 had dropped out, typically because they were overcome by the lure of an especially beloved show. Sad to say, some of these students received very little support on the home front. More than one of them reported having to shield their eyes as they scuttled through rooms where the TV was on or, worse yet, having to eat dinner alone while everyone else ate in front of the set. By the end of the thirty days, a total of 9 more had quit. Two dropped out because they couldn't bear missing out on the family's favorite shows, which everybody else evidently intended to watch. Two others quit because their parents inexplicably chose this moment to purchase new video games for them.[3]

In the end, out of the entire group of 130 students, including those who dropped out, 92 percent claimed they would change their viewing habits: 8 percent said they intended to give up television completely, 41 percent said that they would cut back "a lot" in the future, and 43 percent indicated that they planned to cut back somewhat. The remaining 8 percent said that their viewing habits would remain the same. When asked whether the experiment had been worth it, all of those who had survived the entire thirty days, regardless of what they thought their future viewing habits would be, said that it was. On the last day of the project, two sixth-graders, twin sisters, came up to me with tears in their eyes and told me, "This really was the best month of our lives so far."

101 SCREEN-FREE ACTIVITIES

When the screens are off, it may seem like the only thing left to do is stare at the wall. Fear not! Here are some ideas to get you started on the most fun you've ever had in a month!

Listen to the radio. | Make puppets out of paper bags, old socks, or whatever "junk" you can find. Put on a show! | Paint a picture, a mural, or a room. | Write a story. | Read a book. | Read to someone else. | Investigate your family's history by talking to your older relatives. | Write a letter. | Make cookies, bread, or jam and share with a neighbor. | Read magazines or a newspaper. | Use old magazines and newspapers to make a collage. | Start a diary or journal. | Play cards. | Do some "spring cleaning." | Donate what you don't want or use anymore to Goodwill or have a garage sale. | Do a crossword puzzle. | Wash the car and/or the dog. | Learn about a different culture. Have an international dinner. | Make up a new game with your friends. Teach your family how to play. | Study sign language. | Write a letter to your favorite author. | Read *Dear Mr. Henshaw* by Beverly Cleary. | Cook dinner with friends or family. | Go window shopping. | Attend a religious service. | Walk to work or school. | Make cards for holidays or birthdays. | Play chess, bridge, or checkers. | Play charades. | Have a glass of lemonade and a conversation. | Listen to music and DANCE! | Make a wooden flower box. | Wake up early and make pancakes. | Read a favorite poem. | Learn about the native trees and flowers in your area. | Plan a picnic or barbecue. | Go bird watching. | Walk the dog. | Plant a garden. | Work in your garden. | Take a nature hike. | Feed fish or birds. | Watch the night sky through binoculars; identify different constellations. | Learn to use a compass. | Play hopscotch. | Ride your bike or skateboard. | Go camping. | Go fishing. | Climb a tree. | Watch a sunset. | Attend a community concert. | Visit the library and borrow some books. | Explore the local hobby or craft store. | Visit the animal shelter. | Learn to play a musical instrument. | Go to a museum. | Go roller skating or ice skating. | Go swimming. Join a community swim team. | Start a community group that walks, runs, or bikes. | Visit a skate park. | Have a fashion show. | Learn yoga. | Play soccer, softball, or volleyball. | Play Frisbee. | Take gymnastics. | Take a dance class. | Organize a community clean-up or volunteer for charity. | Help someone younger than you with their reading or math skills. | Join a choir. | Make up silly songs. | Go bowling. | Learn to golf. | Make paper bag costumes and have a parade. | Discover your community center or local park activities. | Blow bubbles. | Make a sidewalk mural with chalk. | Make a calendar. Put a big star on every day you go without screens. | Build a fort in the living room and camp out one night. | Jump rope. Learn to "double dutch." | Start a sticker collection. | Swing on a swing set. | Clean up or redecorate your room. | Make a guitar out of a shoe box and rubber bands. | Make a kazoo out of a comb and a piece of waxed paper. | Start a band. | Construct a kite. Fly it. | Go on a family trip or a historical excursion. | Shoot hoops with friends. | Make a friendship bracelet. | Make a lanyard. | Tell stories around a campfire. | Plan a slumber party. | Construct a miniature boat and float it on water. | Make paper airplanes. | Write a letter to your grandparents. | Make popsicles in an ice cube tray with orange juice and toothpicks. | Organize a neighborhood scavenger hunt. | Play your favorite board games with family or friends. Play Chinese checkers. | Make a sign to tape across the TV to remind everyone how much fun they have without television. | Play hide-and-seek, freeze tag, or telephone. | Sign up for a week at summer camp. | Learn even more things at camp that you can do that are way more fun than television or video games! | **Say "NO!" to your screens!**

—**Bri Sabin, Eastern Washington University student**

Comments from
Teachers and Parents

Teachers observed certain changes in their students over the thirty days. The children seemed to have more energy, as well as a more positive outlook: there was less "grumping around," one said. Teachers remarked as well on the spirit of camaraderie that emerged and the obvious pride the students took in their accomplishment. When, for example, as part of the fourth-grade language arts curriculum, students were asked to describe a great event in their lives, something that had affected them deeply, several wrote about their experience with "30 Days Live." Teachers agreed that the children who participated did better on homework and seemed to develop new interests. They also felt that even the relatively few students who did not take part in the study gained by watching others discover new activities.

On the whole, teachers found it hard to assess how difficult it was for their students to remain "screen free," although one teacher had the impression that her students had an easier time of it as the weeks progressed. The consensus was that the experiment would produce enduring benefits—that it would encourage those who had participated to watch less TV and spend less time with video games. It was clear that taking part in the study had made the children considerably more aware of the place occupied by screen time in their lives and had given them an opportunity to explore alternatives. Several of the teachers guessed, on the basis of the changed behavior they were able to observe in class, that parents had probably had less trouble getting their kids to do chores and homework, and they hoped this would motivate at least some parents to limit their children's TV viewing in the future. They also expressed the hope that because the study offered parents, as well as children, a chance to experience the fun and the value of turning off the TV, parents might make a serious effort to cut back on their own viewing.

I was very conscious of how overburdened teachers are and of the fact that the studies fell during a peak testing period. Yet teachers were unanimous in agreeing not only that the "30 Days Live" experiment was immensely valuable but that it required very little extra work on their part. They generally devoted less than five minutes a day to the project, they reported, usually first thing in the morning, as the students arrived. Regarding the format of

living outside the box

the study, one of the teachers suggested that it would be useful to spend a little more class time, especially at the outset, discussing possible alternatives to television and computer games. It was also suggested that the children's journals be checked at the beginning of the project to make sure the initial quiz had been completed and that parents be asked to sign the journals each week to confirm that the children's reports were accurate. Regarding this last, my only hesitation is that such an approach might tend to turn the project into "homework"—something an authority figure is checking up on. One goal of the study was to encourage children to develop their own motivation, and so it seemed important to give them a chance to be responsible and trustworthy of their own accord.

All the parents whose children had taken part in the study, regardless of whether their child had lasted one day or all thirty, were asked to fill out a short survey, consisting of seven questions, at the conclusion of the study. A little under half of them returned the questionnaire. Interestingly, the parents were evenly divided as to whether the experiment grew easier as time wore on. Half reported that, as the thirty days progressed, it became increasingly difficult to keep their children away from the TV and other screens; the other half said that the first few days were the hardest. However, all agreed that the experiment was well worth the effort, even if it presented certain challenges at home. As one parent summed it up: "It was a tough experiment, but good!" The fact that fewer than half the parents bothered to complete the questionnaire is nonetheless troubling. One would hope that even the parents of children who did not manage to last the entire thirty days would have enough interest in the project, and enough pride in their child's willingness to make an effort, that they could take a few minutes to complete a questionnaire. Again, one wonders whether parents' own investment in television—their reluctance to face the TV issue head on, especially if this would entail modifying their own behavior—made it difficult for some of them to get behind such a project wholeheartedly. It is all too easy to imagine a parent dismissing the undertaking as just another burdensome school-related task, all the more onerous because it threatened to disrupt home routines.

That said, a number of the parents who did return the questionnaire specifically called attention to the beneficial impact of the study on home

DINNER CONVERSATION STARTERS

*Sometimes it's hard to know what to talk about around the dinner table,
especially if you are used to watching television while you eat.
Here are some ideas to get you talking!*

"What was the best part of your day? The challenges?"

"What made you laugh today?"

"Describe how you would decorate your room, if cost was not an issue."

"What would life be like if we had no words to communicate with?"

"What has been your favorite age in your life? Why?"

Play "Would you rather . . ." by asking either/or questions: "Would you
rather be too hot or too cold?" "Would you rather cry cottage cheese or
sweat glue?" "Would you rather have ice cubes for hands or not be able
to tell the difference between a baby and a muffin?" "Would you rather
be blind or deaf?" Have everyone explain the "why" of their answer.

"What have been the five best things in your life so far?"

"If you could meet anyone—living, dead, or even fictional—who would
it be? What would you do together? What would you talk about?"

"Who inspires you in life?"

"List the five most important qualities a friend should have. How about
a parent? A teacher?"

"If you woke up one morning to find that you suddenly knew how to play
an instrument of your choosing, what instrument would it be?"

"Are you more of a VW Beetle or a Ferrari?"

"Describe what the Earth will be like in fifty years. What about in a thousand years?"

"What is the best thing you can do for a friend?"

living outside the box

life. "It was really peaceful in the house," commented one, who felt that turning off the TV was "definitely a boost for family harmony." Another echoed these sentiments: "Even though the other children did not quit watching, I noticed the TV was turned on less, and the house was much more peaceful." Another added: "We all got more sleep, and the girls got more exercise." Parents also noticed that the absence of TV promoted conversation—or, as one of them put it, "My child was a lot more talkative!" Another parent reported: "Without TV, my daughter and I used the time to talk more. She also said her mood was better without all of the 'icky' commercials." For at least one mother, though, the tendency toward greater interaction had its downside: "At times it was frustrating because my daughter would stick pretty close to me," she commented. "I enjoy my space too!"

Much as teachers had predicted, several of the parents remarked that the "30 Days Live" experience had made them more conscious of the role of television in their own lives. "Weekends were very hard," one of them admitted; "that habit of turning the TV on in the mornings is hard to overcome!" "We noticed that TV is a big time-eater and that less is better," commented another, while a third promised, "I will be more aware of TV from now on and not always turn it on—thanks!" Of the parents who completed the questionnaire, roughly two-thirds predicted that their children's viewing habits would change as a result of their participation in the study, and nearly half of them felt that the entire family would end up watching less television in the future.

Those of us involved in organizing "30 Days Live" had originally assumed that relatively few children would be able to last the entire period. So we were happily surprised when such a large percentage survived for the full month, particularly because many of them did so in the absence of overwhelming support at home. It was rewarding to see how quickly "30 Days Live" became a kid-driven project. The high success rate is proof that even among an unusually vulnerable segment of our population—one targeted by TV producers and video game manufacturers—the habit can be broken. Moreover, the strongly positive sentiments that these children expressed in weekly interview sessions are evidence that, far from complaining incessantly or becoming listless and depressed, if

SCREEN-FREE BIRTHDAY PARTY IDEAS

Long, long ago, in a not-so-distant past, the idea of playing video games or watching movies at a birthday party seemed awfully boring. Here are some fun, screen-free ideas for your next birthday party. They are sure to make it the best birthday ever!

- Have a build-your-own sundae bar, complete with ice cream, chocolate syrup, and all the toppings you can think of.
- Go "retro." Have everyone arrive in 1980s-style clothes. Go roller-skating or ice skating looking "tubular."
- Take your friends to your local pool or aquatic center for a pool party.
- Have a few friends go with you to Wild Walls and spend the day rock climbing.
- Have an outdoor scavenger hunt. Start by making a list of fifteen or twenty small items. Then split your guests into two or more groups, and give each group a copy of the list and a bag in which to place their finds.
- Make your birthday last a whole weekend or more: take your family and a few friends camping.
- No girls' slumber party is complete without makeovers! See how fabulous (or silly!) you can make each other look.
- Go bowling! At some alleys, "cosmic bowling" starts early enough in the evening for you and your friends to bowl under black lights and laser shows.
- Birthday party standards like "Pin the Tail on the Donkey" or musical chairs just get funnier as you get older.
- Go to the park and play a giant game of "Capture the Flag." Use water balloons to "tag" each other!
- Bust out a game like Jenga or Cranium. If you have a lot of guests, make two or more games available at once.
- Have a tropical-themed party, complete with tiki torches and fruit skewers. Go running through the sprinkler. Hand out colored paper and yarn for your guests to make leis to wear.
- Backyard campouts can be the most fun sleepover parties. Sleep out under the stars, tell stories, and have your parents help you make banana boats on the barbecue! (Recipe for a banana boat: 1 banana slit length-wise, stuffed with chocolate chips and minimarshmallows. Wrap in aluminum foil—shiny side in!—and cook on the barbecue until banana is soft.)

For more fun party ideas, have your parents visit www.familyfun.com or just use your imagination. You'd be surprised at what you can come up with on your own. Remember, "30 Days Live" is about REALLY living . . . not just pumping blood!

children are given a taste of life without television, they will be intrigued and on the whole adapt without much trouble.

What Children Have to Tell Us

On the final day of the "30 Days Live" project, Mitchell, the fourth-grader who never made it beyond the first night, said, "I think that '30 Days Live' is a good thing. If you didn't watch TV, you might see more of your family and do more stuff." Some of the children of parents who responded to my earlier survey of TV-free families also offered an assessment of life without television. For instance, I heard from Keisha, age ten, and Sally, age twelve. "I find that reading is much faster and funner than TV," Keisha reported. "TV can get too gory. And it can get too childish. I much prefer books in any case. Besides, I don't know what the big deal is. There are about a million other fun things to do besides sitting and watching something." Sally added, "I don't know how I'd ever have any time for TV. I'm in the sixth grade, I have eight classes, and I'm loaded with homework every day including weekends. I also take karate twice a week, horseback riding on Saturdays, and violin on Sundays. I barely have any free time. When I do have free time (that's like never), I like to swim in the pool, ride my bike, spend time with my cat, and read, write, or draw—I'm like any normal kid, just without the TV. It isn't one of those things on my list and doesn't seem that appealing to me."

Fiona, a teenager, believed that growing up without TV had "forced" her to find other amusements such as reading, writing, baking, and playing piano. After the TV made its exit, she wrote, "I think my mom 'sprinkled' books and craft ideas around the house. I would be so bored that I would pick one of them up and soon be completely absorbed. She planted books of every kind, and I read them all. I also played imagination games galore without TV programs to shape them." But that was not all. "The media has had much less effect on the way I feel about my body and how I look," she continued. "I think outside of more boxes—what is considered popular and such, and how I should be if I want to fit in. I hear most kids see 200,000 violent acts on TV by the time they're eighteen years old. I guess I missed all of them. For the most part I don't even think about my family not having a TV, and I doubt I would watch it very much if we did."

In response to a question about the changes brought about by going TV free, seventeen-year-old Ben summed up his experience this way: "I've grown up without a TV, so my life hasn't really changed as much as it has been shaped by the lack of television. I've never wanted or cared about different brands of anything, and I've never wanted a toy or game that I hadn't seen in action and liked. I've felt a bit disconnected from some of my peers because they always talked about TV stuff that I had no experience of. I can't easily recognize the names of various actors or TV programs. I picked up reading early on and still really enjoy reading. I don't feel I am that different—I just read more than the average kid does. That's how I get my information."

When my own daughter, Sydney, was eleven, she wrote an essay about growing up without television. As she explained, when friends ask her, "How can you live without TV?" she tells them it's easy. "All you really need is an imagination. When I was little, I would sit at the top of our couch with a wooden pole and an old tie of my dad's tied to it, pretending I was fishing. I also used to make millions of tiny little paper books. I would line up all of my stuffed animals along the wall and give them a school lesson. Occasionally we would have tea parties. Obviously I don't do that any more, but I am involved in many sports, and I have friends over all the time. I also play the flute, the saxophone, and the piano. I have my share of fun and my share of chores. Honestly, if we did have a TV, I don't think I'd have time to watch any."

Family Investments   Rather ironically, one of my own fond memories of childhood involves the TV set. When I was growing up—at a time when most families owned only one television, which received three channels—my family used to gather around the TV once a week to watch Disney's *Sunday Night Movies*. We spread out the pillows, my mom popped popcorn and sliced apples, and my dad scooped vanilla ice cream into tall glasses and poured Grapette soda on top. I don't remember the shows. What I remember is being together. Even more memorable than *Sunday Night Movies*, though, were the nights when a winter blizzard was brewing around our Iowa farm and the power went out. My parents lit the kerosene lamp and stoked up the fire in the grate, and we dug out the sandwich maker and played games by firelight, my brother and I fervently praying that the school buses would be buried in deep drifts by morning. What made a powerful and lasting imprint on my young mind was being in the same room, focusing on a common activity, creating an experience that we would share in memory.

Leo Tolstoy once wrote, "From age five to eighty is but a step. From birth to age five is an appalling distance." Researchers tell us that a truly phenomenal amount of learning takes place during the first five years of life. Brain cells develop in explosive proportions, and children begin modeling adult behavior and forming lifelong habits. During those early years, and well beyond, family relationships form a kind of protective shield against distress, despair, and folly. Children remember the games they played, the family traditions, and the sense of belonging and security they felt, and it helps to remind them who they are. The time families spend together during a child's formative years becomes a long-term investment, not unlike money in a savings account, the benefits gradually compounding. The earlier the investment is made, the greater it grows over the years. Eventually it may be drawn upon for support during difficult times, as well as for pleasure when times are good.

Sadly, though, opportunities for family bonding are becoming increasingly scarce, and the way people behave within families and the assumptions they make about what constitutes standard family patterns have changed dramatically. Perhaps some families still watch certain special programs together, but more often than not we are off in our own rooms absorbed with our own favorite shows. Instead of bringing families together, as it was once predicted television would, TV has alienated us from one another and from the family rituals that serve as models for a well-integrated life, one in which time to oneself is balanced by time spent in contact with others. Although the time consumed by television on any single day may seem relatively small, the minutes and hours add up. In the end, they equal years of isolation—lifetimes of conversations that never took place and possibilities that were never pursued. If you're reading this book, chances are you're not one of the helpless prisoners to the four-plus-hours-a-day habit. But even if your TV viewing appears to be well under control, it doesn't hurt to ask occasionally whether this is how those minutes might best be used.

Jack Mingo, author of *The Official Couch Potato Handbook*, once reported that when children between the ages of four and six were asked which they preferred, spending time with their fathers or watching TV, better than half—54 percent—chose TV.[4] Many years later, a young boy who, along with many of his classmates, had just taken part in National TV-Turnoff Week commented, "I played card games with my dad for the very first time." One can only wonder, then, what the 54 percent of children who said they'd rather watch TV than spend time with dad had ever actually *done* with their fathers. Even playing a simple card game demands concentration and decision making—but, above all, it involves interaction: conversation, teasing, laughter. Think what our children might learn, how they might grow, if they had a chance to do some of the things they aren't doing because instead they're staring at a screen. What dreams might come true, what relationships become richer? Children are born to search, explore, invent, manipulate, fix, build, fantasize, climb trees, run, and roll in the grass. But at the moment they have run out of time in which to do all this.

8: breaking the soft addiction

In its easy provision of relaxation and escape, television can be beneficial in limited doses. Yet when the habit interferes with the ability to grow, to learn new things, to lead an active life, then it constitutes dependence and should be taken seriously.

—Robert Kubey and Mihaly Csikszentmihalyi,
"Television Addiction Is No Mere Metaphor"

The jury is finally in. Television can now be considered a genuine addiction. Writing in the February 2002 issue of *Scientific American*, Robert Kubey and Mihaly Csikszentmihalyi argue that, although "imprecise and laden with value judgments," the notion of TV addiction "captures the essence of a very real phenomenon."[1] They cite the following criteria, to which psychiatrists and social workers refer in defining substance abuse:

- we spend a great deal of time using the substance
- we use it more often than we intend
- we think about reducing our use or make repeated unsuccessful efforts to do so
- we give up important social, family, or occupational activities in order to use the substance, and
- we experience withdrawal symptoms when we stop using the substance.

Millions of TV-watching Americans exhibit these five signs of addiction. In moderate doses, of course, television can be a pleasure like many others. The trick is to limit our viewing—to resist the temptation to keep watching. As Kubey and Csikszentmihalyi put it, "Television can teach and amuse; it can reach aesthetic heights; it can provide much needed distraction and escape. The difficulty arises when people strongly sense that they ought not to watch as much as they do and yet are unable to reduce their viewing."[2]

Understanding TV's Attraction

In 1992, an article in *Health* magazine reported that nearly half of all American adults (49 percent) claimed they wished they watched less television.[3] Chances are a similar percentage would say the same today. So what's stopping us? The answer may lie partly with the TV screen itself. As we all know, a TV set exerts enormous powers of visual attraction. Kubey and Csikszentmihalyi suggest that the reason may have to do with a biological "orienting response," first described in 1927 by Ivan Pavlov. An orienting response, which originally served to help the human species detect possible danger, is an "instinctive visual or auditory reaction to any sudden or novel stimulus," in the course of which "the brain focuses its attention on gathering more information while the rest of the body quiets."[4] We have probably all had the experience of passing through a room or an aisle in a department store and finding our eyes automatically drawn to the images on a television. Our attention is captivated, and soon we are absorbed in the plot or caught up in a discussion or news item. Even if we are not especially interested in what we are watching, we may have difficulty tearing ourselves away.

But if our biological heritage can perhaps explain why a TV set automatically commands our attention, our fondness for television likely owes more to the fact that it helps us relax—that is, to the influence it has on our mood. At least to some degree, the effects of television on mood can be studied physiologically, for example, by using an electroencephalograph to examine changes in brain waves. But the complexities of emotion exceed our present capacity to describe them by purely mechanical measures. In an effort to capture the subjective subtleties of mood, Mihaly Csikszentmihalyi developed an approach called the Experience Sampling Method (ESM), in which subjects report directly on their emotional state. Participants in ESM studies carry a beeper by which they are prompted six to eight times a day to record what they are doing and how they are feeling. Not surprisingly, such studies reveal that people tend to feel relaxed and passive while they are watching television. This state of relaxation sets in almost immediately when the TV is turned on, and it ends fairly abruptly when the set is turned off. Interestingly, however, what Kubey and Csikszentmihalyi described as "feelings of passivity and lowered alertness" persist, leaving the viewer feeling emotionally and even physically depleted. In fact, participants in ESM studies often report that the longer they spend watching TV, the less satisfaction they derive from watching. Subjects also frequently note that they have greater difficulty concentrating on something after watching TV.[5]

Much like television, habit-forming drugs bring about improvements in mood, and the more swiftly the drug takes effect, the more addictive it is likely to be. But the user's mood deteriorates, sometimes quite dramatically, as the drug wears off, and so users are tempted to continue taking the drug. Similarly, because the relaxation produced by television is only temporary, viewers tend to keep watching. Moreover, although television is visually stimulating, it is not mentally stimulating, as measures of the alpha waves in our brains indicate. It draws us into a state of passivity and leaves us feeling vaguely anaesthetized. In contrast, activities that involve greater mental stimulation, such as reading or pursuing a hobby, or that generate endorphins, such as engaging in sports, also improve mood and produce a sense of relaxation, but the effects appear to last long after the activity itself is completed.

Symptoms of Addiction   In short, we associate television with more or less instant relaxation, and we continue watching it because we want to hang onto that state of relaxation—because experience tells us that we will feel less relaxed if we stop watching. But what about long-term psychological effects? Does all that relaxation mean that those who spend hours in front of the set gradually experience reduced levels of stress? Apparently not. In ESM research studies, heavy TV viewers reported feeling "significantly more anxious and less happy than light viewers [did] in unstructured situations, such as doing nothing, daydreaming, or waiting in line."[6] When the viewer was alone, the differences were even more apparent. One fascinating study, carried out some three decades ago, looked at a mountain community in which television was nonexistent until the advent of cable. Over time, residents of the community became "less creative in problem solving, less able to persevere at tasks, and less tolerant of unstructured time." Other researchers have argued that individuals who watch large amounts of television may suffer from decreased patience and self-restraint and shorter attention spans.[7] Over the long haul, TV addicts thus appear to react much like other addicts, who are often edgy or irritable when they are not actively using their substance of choice and have nothing else with which to distract themselves.

Another study, one that a colleague and I conducted, looked at a group of 750 adults divided equally according to their established patterns of TV viewing. A third of these individuals watched no television at all, another third watched a maximum of two hours a day, and the remaining third more than two hours. The participants were asked to complete a series of psychosocial tests designed to measure loneliness, shyness, self-esteem, boredom, and body concept. Those who watched no TV scored the highest on the tests, although their scores were only slightly better than those of the individuals whose viewing was limited to no more than two hours daily. When it came to those who watched in excess of two hours each day, however, scores plummeted significantly across all the psychosocial measures.[8]

Yet the fact remains that, despite the many negative effects associated with heavy TV viewing, for most of the population the pull of the screen is hard to resist. No doubt the promise of short-term relaxation is powerful enough to outweigh concerns about long-term consequences, much as a smoker who wants a cigarette is unlikely to be deterred by a list of statistics about lung cancer. Of course, the main reason an addict wants a fix is that without it he or she will begin to experience withdrawal symptoms. Anyone who has tried to stop smoking will tell you how swiftly one's resolve melts away when the craving for a cigarette kicks in. Those who study addiction talk about "triggers"—specific situations or conditions that are associated with using, such as the cocktail hour or, for a smoker, that first cup of morning coffee. Similar triggers exist for TV viewers: arriving home from work or school, for instance, or knowing that a favorite show is about to come on. *Not* to turn on the TV under such circumstances—to forgo that promise of instant relaxation—can produce anxiety, irritation, a sense of loss or loneliness, and other symptoms of distress. In response to a dare, a good friend of mine decided to give TV-Turnoff Week a try. He told me that when he arrived home from work on the first day and was greeted by empty TV screens staring at him from several rooms, he literally got the shakes. In desperation, he took refuge in the garage, where he ended up spending several hours doing some much-needed reorganizing (quite a satisfying activity, he reported).

Curiously, relatively little systematic research has been devoted to the symptoms of withdrawal from television, although, over the years, power outages and broken TV sets have yielded occasional insights. Some forty years ago, Gary Steiner, a professor at the University of Chicago, charted the responses of a few individuals whose televisions had broken. "Screamed constantly," was one comment; "children bothered me, and my nerves were on edge." Or, as one woman declared: "It was terrible. We did nothing"—and, in the same breath, "My husband and I talked."[9] In other studies, people were offered a nominal fee to go without TV for a week or a month. Even with that incentive, however, many could not complete the required period of abstinence, and some even claimed they fought, verbally and physically. At the same time, as Kubey and Csikszentmihalyi point out, "Researchers have yet to flesh out these anecdotes; no one has systematically gathered statistics on the prevalence of these withdrawal symptoms."[10]

Nevertheless, many researchers see the existence of withdrawal symptoms as the most convincing parallel between TV and addictive behavior. Some viewers try to cut back on their habit but fail, try again and fail, then try again and perhaps succeed for a while, only to lapse back into their old habits. Then they try again—and so on, over and over. Then again, there are those who *do* succeed in substantially reducing the amount of time they spend in front of the set or who manage to break the TV habit altogether. The reasons why some succeed while others seem doomed to endless struggle are many and varied, but one major factor would appear to be an individual's willingness to cope with symptoms of withdrawal.

Withdrawal from TV: Firsthand Reports

TV addicts are inclined to assume that attempting to live without their drug of choice would simply prove too difficult—that the withdrawal period would be too traumatic. And yet evidence suggests that addiction to TV is in fact a fairly easy habit to break, provided the person is prepared to make a sincere effort. Reports from those who have made the transition suggest that adapting to life without TV seldom entails major emotional upheaval and can occur in a relatively short time.

In the spring of 2001, I undertook a project intended in part to gather information about withdrawal from television. For several weeks prior to National TV-Turnoff Week, in April, I ran an online announcement soliciting volunteers for a three-month-long "Cold-Turkey Turnoff" that would begin with TV-Turnoff Week itself. Volunteers were asked at the outset to describe their current viewing habits and then to submit descriptive email reports at the end of the first and second weeks and again at the end of the second and third months. There were no other requirements, and participation was entirely voluntary: if a report failed to arrive from someone, I did not contact the person myself.

At the close of the study, those taking part were asked to sum up their experience by completing a short questionnaire. They were asked what their biggest discovery had been and whether particular aspects of their life—fitness, relationship with spouse or significant other, relationship with children, mental outlook, sleeping habits, and so on—had improved. They were also asked whether they felt they had missed out on anything during the twelve weeks and were invited to describe the negative aspects of the experience. The questions also included: "What were the circumstances (if any) that made you fall 'off the wagon'?" "What would you say were the top three things you did to replace TV in your life during the past twelve weeks?" "How do you now plan to deal with TV in

living outside the box

your life?" and "What advice would you give to others who are considering watching less TV?" At the request of some of the participants, the project was repeated in 2002.

For the most part, the initial viewing habits of the participants were unremarkable. Rebecca and Scott, for example, who were averaging 29 hours per week, said they watched a few favorite shows on weekday evenings, while on Friday nights and weekends they usually rented movies. Their kids watched TV from about 3:30 to 5:30 p.m. Mondays through Fridays and some four to six hours of videos on weekends. Steve—who, at 21 hours per week, came in a little under the national average—had grown up watching several hours of TV a day, but he had quit while in college. Now married, he had fallen back into his old habits. He said that he was motivated to try the Cold-Turkey Turnoff because of some of the conversations he had found himself having at work. "We were talking about people on shows we watch like they were people we knew, like the stuff on TV was part of our real lives, and I decided it had gone too far," he explained. "It was kind of frightening. I can see now why people say TV is leading to the decline of our society. Even if you don't watch that much, when you start to feel you know a fictional character way better than your next-door neighbor, something is seriously wrong."

Among the participants were also some who qualified as quite heavy viewers. Mike, who was watching about 35 hours a week, felt he was wasting his life. "I wasn't reaching out to people for relationships—and being single, that isn't good," he commented. "I wasn't assessing what needed to be done. I would get into the easy chair and watch the news and then stay a few extra hours watching sitcoms. What a way to see your life slip away." Cheryl—who went on to survive the entire three months—was averaging about 36 hours a week at the start of the study. She said her day generally began with about two hours of television in the early morning. Maybe twice a week, when she came home for lunch, she would watch another thirty minutes or so. In early evening, after she got home, she would relax in front of the TV for about an hour, and then later, during prime time, she would add anywhere from one hour to three hours more, depending on what was on that night. "I didn't even have cable," she admitted, "and I managed to watch that much TV. Yuck."

The First Two Weeks　　　　In 2001, a grand total of twenty-one brave souls volunteered for the Cold-Turkey Turnoff. Here are some representative samples of what participants had to report at the end of their first full week without television:

- At the beginning of the week I was definitely missing TV. But as the week went by, I really didn't miss it. I found out that it's much easier to keep up with schoolwork—I'm in college, studying to be an elementary schoolteacher. Thursday night, my husband wanted to watch *E.R.* We agreed no, but it was a little tough, especially since the next day in the cafeteria line I overheard two people talking about what a great episode it was. We ended up in a great philosophical discussion about the (de)merits of getting so involved in fictitious characters on TV and about how literature is so different (no commercials!). My husband and I also helped plan a "Family Game Night" in honor of National TV-Turnoff Week at our local elementary school. I even taught an African-American dance to some students and their parents!

- I have been TV free for one week! It has been easier than I thought it would be, besides those brief moments of temptation when I sit down and really want to lose myself in mind-obliterating numbness. The hardest moment this past week was on Thursday. The U.S. Men's National Soccer Team had a World Cup qualifier, and I really wanted to watch. Or at least get updates as to the score. But since our country is so soccer backward, I couldn't find the game on the radio or even on the Internet. But I survived, and so did the soccer team. They won out against Costa Rica, 1–0.

- This has been a very busy week for me at school, so I wasn't home as much in the evenings, and that made it easier to not watch TV. I definitely felt the urge to turn the TV on when I first got home from school so I could veg out for an hour to unwind. But after about ten minutes of really missing TV, I got over it and found something else to do.

　　　　　　　　　　　　　living outside the box

- We finished our first ever TV-free week. Hooray! As a single mom, I wasn't sure how it would go, but what a difference it made to be "boob tube" free for my kids, Jon, thirteen, Dave, eleven, and Abigail, seven. The older boy's first reaction was: "What! No TV for three months? We'll do it for one week but not for twelve, Mom!" My youngest thought it could be fun. . . . We are taking it one week at a time. I personally don't miss it. Well, except maybe *Touched by an Angel* and the new series on PAX 34, *Doc*, and some shows on PBS. Hmmm . . . I guess I watched more than I thought!
- This has been a good experience so far. Turning the TV off and keeping it off has been much easier than I expected. Going into this, I sort of planned on "relapsing" to watch *Survivor*, but I found that when Thursday came, I wasn't even interested. The biggest difference I've noticed is time. Not just the fact that I have more time, but that time itself is structured so differently. Before it was always, "Oh, ten o'clock, this is on," or "I've gotta be home at 8:30 to see that." Now I find that I can do things when I want for as long as I'd like.

Maria, the single mother, said that she caught her children watching TV only twice during the first week. "Video games are still a struggle to turn off—for instance, Game Boy," she reported, although she also commented that her children "are doing better now and are getting into the habit of making up something to do, whether it's fun or work." In her estimation, her two boys "found not watching TV easier than they thought." In addition, Maria provided a list of the positive developments she noticed during her family's first week without television:

- More kid-initiated conversations with parent
- Each family member is calmer and friendlier toward the others
- Definitely more time to play board games or anything else
- Less sound pollution from TV
- More reaching out to friends by phone

- Easier to do school homework with no TV magnet to distract
- More time for outdoors play, especially now when there's no snow
- More time for mom to unclutter and organize the house.

Not surprisingly, certain familiar themes were heard in the end-of-the-first-week reports. Participants found themselves confronted with various "trigger" situations. They were tempted by their favorite shows or by the desire to unwind in front of the television, or they felt momentarily at a loss at times when, according to their established routine, they would have turned the TV on. Interestingly, though, these moments of temptation seldom seemed to last very long. As soon as participants shifted their attention to some other activity, thoughts of television faded away. Again and again I was told that resisting TV's pull was "easier than I expected."

Of course, there were those who yielded to temptation. "I lasted one whole week," Dave wrote, "and then *The Sopranos* made me an offer I couldn't refuse." His relapse notwithstanding, Dave did not altogether abandon his resolve. "I will attempt to keep TV viewing to a minimum," he added, "as I'm enjoying getting more reading done." Another fellow, who quit at the end of TV-Turnoff Week itself, nonetheless called his TV-free week "a wonderful idea that gave me a new beginning." He planned to downgrade his cable TV service, he said, from one that provided him with upwards of a hundred channels (for about $50 a month) to one that would provide only local broadcast channels (for only $10 a month). "I don't think I'll miss the mindless surfing of an endless channel lineup," he remarked.

Aside from comments about temptation, which I had anticipated, I was struck by something else as I read the participants' first-week reports. Although one must guard against the impulse to read too much into a handful of anecdotal comments, it seemed to me that, after only seven days, a certain shift of emphasis was already underway. The feeling of loss, of something being missing, was beginning to give way to a sense of discovery, primarily of the fact that eliminating television frees up time for other activities. By the end of the second week, the change was even more apparent: enthusiasm was growing. Participants talked about exploring new pursuits or rediscovering old ones. "My household is fast becoming

living outside the box

NPR fanatics," wrote Jason, the soccer fan. "And who can deny that NPR is the best source of news and interesting programs in this country (and in this galaxy)?" Scott noted that living without television "has given me the chance to revisit my CD collection, much of which has gone untouched lately," adding that "as this goes on, and summer approaches, I hope to spend my newfound extra time outdoors with my wife." Cheryl informed me that, during the first week, she had been tempted to turn the TV on at mealtimes: "I used to find myself migrating to the living room with my food." But, she continued, "this week I sat and read at the table instead. That has seemed to work just fine. I've been paying more attention to the house, meaning that I'm keeping up with the dishes and cleaning. I've also felt the urge to draw a lot more—not sure if it's a coincidence or if it has something to do with no TV. I'm going strong and looking forward to what creativity emerges in the coming weeks."

In addition, several of the participants remarked on the impact of their decision on others. "I was at my parents' house a few times this week," Steve reported, "and they are avid TV watchers. But when I told them I was doing the turnoff, they made an attempt to limit the time the TV was on, and I think it gave us some time to do things we don't always do, like play cards. . . . I thought it was cool they gave the TV a rest." Similarly, Jason commented: "One nice result of not watching TV is that when I enter a room where people are watching TV, those who know that I am trying to give it up will turn it off. Whether this is out of courtesy or in the name of good conversation I do not know. So I am inadvertently changing the TV viewing habits of others." The fact that both these individuals were prepared to be upfront about what they were trying to accomplish is a measure of their dedication to the project—and both were clearly pleased to think that their decision to forgo television was having an influence on others.

Second- and Third-Month Survivors Out of the twenty-one volunteers who began the Cold-Turkey Turnoff, only fourteen survived to turn in reports at the end of the second week—an attrition rate of one in three. By the end of the second month, however, twelve out of the fourteen were still hanging in there. Again, it is difficult to generalize on the basis of such a small sample, but this pattern does seems to suggest something. Going without television for a relatively brief period, such as a week, is a challenge, to be sure, but it is a finite challenge. Every year, for example, several million people take a vacation from TV by participating in TV-Turnoff Week. The hope is, of course, that the experience will motivate at least some of the participants to pursue longer-term change. All the same, those taking part in the event can comfort themselves with the thought that, if they so choose, they can turn the TV on again at the end of the week. To decide instead to prolong the experiment is evidence of a serious interest in replacing one lifestyle with another, perhaps permanently, or at least in exploring that possibility—and to accomplish such a goal requires a much firmer commitment. Perhaps, then, for those withdrawing from television, getting through a second week, rather than the first, is the real test of that commitment.

What did come through loud and clear in the reports I received at the end of the second month was that, after just eight weeks, the survivors were growing pretty comfortable with their TV-free life. They spoke of the new activities they had discovered (or the old ones they had rediscovered) and repeatedly commented that they no longer missed television. One couple sent this report:

> We have been having so much fun without TV that we are not around long enough to check our email! We do not even miss our favorite television program, *The Simpsons*. I think we've all forgotten what was going on in the other shows anyway. The TV remains out of our living room and in the back room but did emerge twice so that we could watch a rented video. We live in a rural area with not much choice in movie theaters, and it is so expensive to go to a theater, so we rented twice and dug out the TV/VCR unit from the back room. But we didn't plug in the antenna to the rest of TV land.
>
> Since our life with TV has ceased we have enjoyed many good books, leisurely dinners (not hurrying through them so that we don't miss a TV program), lots of radio and album

playing, guitar, flute, singing, and more time for gardening, walking, and biking.

I would not have dreamed this two months ago, but bad TV has left our household, and I don't think it is ever coming back. I don't even miss the weather channel anymore—it was usually wrong anyway! Thanks for this opportunity to challenge ourselves to go "cold turkey" from TV.

I was pleased to hear from Cheryl, who likewise seemed to be going strong:

At the end of the second month, I no longer long to watch TV or get bored with big chunks of free time. Instead of waking up to and going to bed with TV, I read a bit in the mornings during breakfast and then read a bit more to unwind in the evenings. The sewing machine is fixed, and I've taught myself to crochet—currently working on an afghan! I can't remember a time in my life when I've been so productive.

The best thing to come out of this whole experience is that I like how I don't want to watch TV anymore, and I no longer care what's going on with different TV shows. When I'm at friends' houses with the TV on, it's hard to watch it. At first I get drawn in, but then I become irritated and overwhelmed. If I leave the room, I feel better. Now, when friends come over, we don't sit around watching TV—we do "stuff." I've taught a friend to sew, and now we spend our time together doing that.

I also received this message, from a woman who had not previously contacted me:

I participated in TV-Turnoff Week this year, and then I found out about the Cold-Turkey Turnoff. So I decided to join in. After that first week, I had absolutely no desire to turn the TV back on. In honor of TV-Turnoff Week I decided to read Jerry Mander's *Four Arguments for the Elimination of Television*, and after that I read Neil Postman's *Amusing Ourselves to Death*. I found both books extremely thought provoking and fascinating. I had done quite a bit of reading in grad school, but after graduation I decided to take a break—that stretched into three years! Turning off the TV and reading those two books helped me to remember how much more I get out of reading than watching television. I prefer to be mentally stimulated, as well as challenged. I loved school. How, I asked myself, did I ever let myself fall into such a rut? Turning the TV off helped me to rediscover my love of books and of learning.

This young woman also appended a rather insightful list of the "revelations" that had come to her as a result of her TV-free experience thus far. Among them were:

- Giving up television is easier to do with a friend (my boyfriend also turned the TV off)
- Giving up television makes you aware of how ubiquitous it is
- *All* television content is advertising, not just the commercials. Television programs teach us how we should look, dress, think, and behave. Since I have been exposed mainly to real people, without their own personal makeup and hair artists, my desire for shiny and bouncy hair and a flawless complexion has markedly diminished.
- A nation full of ardent TV viewers has contributed to a discontented society, since we realize we'll never have the clothes, looks, homes, cars, friends, free time, or thirty-minute-solvable problems that our "friends" on TV have
- Spending the time I used to spend vegging in front of the TV on other activities, such as nature walks, reading, and stimulating conversations, has proven to be a much more fulfilling way of life.

By the end of the third month, the transition appeared largely to be complete. The initial disorientation of withdrawal had given way to a sense of satisfaction, and those who had lasted the three months seemed at ease with their new way of life. Some were clearly "converts." Sally and Rob—the couple who had brought the TV out of cold storage in order to watch a couple of movies—wrote: "We've still got the television in its storage location, have really enjoyed being without television, and do not plan on letting it back into our lives. We hope the others who did the Cold-Turkey Turnoff have enjoyed the new freedom we have." Cheryl claimed that she was "surprised" to have made it through the entire three months. She admitted that at first "I really wanted to watch TV. It would call to me, and I would consciously have to put it out of my mind." But as she went on to report:

> Now I don't think about it at all. I also noticed how the time between emails to you felt as if it shortened. The first two weeks, it seemed like time was dragging, but this last month flew by. I couldn't believe it was time to write again. I've been so busy living life. The evenings are no longer wasted on veg-ging out anymore. I've read more than ever and made a lot of clothing during these three months. My husband and I have talked more in the past two months than in the past two years! Thank you for hosting this challenge. I hope you do it again next year so I can tell others to give it a try.

At the end of the three months, participants were asked what they thought they had learned from the experience. "That even super, interest-ing, and fun programs should not take precedence over 'the important things' in life," one replied. Another wrote: "I missed TV and didn't miss it at the same time. I missed the news. And PBS, TLC, and the Discovery Channel, and, well, the Outdoor Life network. But overall I didn't miss the inane drama and sitcoms. Like my friend said after trying life as a veg-etarian, 'I discovered that meat doesn't have to be the main course at every meal.' I also feel like TV doesn't have to be the centerpiece of life outside work. I read and listen to the news a lot more. I now enjoy the freedom and breadth of coverage of the Internet, radio, and print much more than the mainstream conservatism of television."

One couple reported that they had intentionally relapsed at the end of the three months, only to make an unexpected discovery. "After three months without TV," they told me, "we turned on our favorite program, *The Simpsons*. The program seemed so short, with so much time devoted to commercials. It drove us crazy! Half of them were for other shows, and the other half for cell phones and other superfluous items. Thirty minutes for one program wore us out, and we were bored. When it was over, we realized how much time we had wasted when we each could have been pursuing another project." Another participant said that she and her husband would no doubt continue to rent the occasional video, "and I'm sure I will relapse into TV zombiehood the next time I have a bout of the flu." But, she continued, "other than that, we are too busy doing all the other cool stuff we discovered we liked."

Quite a few of the participants remarked on the fact that, once the TV was turned off, time seemed to expand. One woman said she was struck by "how long my days became. I could accomplish more in a single TV-free day than I would have in several when I watched TV, often wasting three to six hours a day." Her comment was echoed by another "graduate" who wrote: "I can't believe the amount of things I can get done in one day. In the time I would take to watch TV in the evening, I can now read a book for an hour, go for a walk, meet with friends, and work on some art. This is perfect for me because I have a hard time staying with one thing for a long period of time. Now I can do all sorts of things in one day. I love it. I feel pretty damn good."

Trials and Tribulations   Roughly three-quarters of the participants in the Cold-Turkey Turnoff commented at some point during the three months that withdrawing from TV was easier than they had anticipated. To the extent that they had a tough time, it tended to be in the evenings, when the pull of TV was the strongest, whether because a favorite show was about to come on or because they were accustomed to using TV to relax and to fill up "empty" time. As Cheryl reported, "At first, I experienced extreme boredom during the withdrawal period. The time of the day when I would most feel the pressure was in the evening, when I would get a strong urge to turn the TV on. It was hard to ignore that urge. For years I watched TV in the evening when I was done with the things I had to do that day. To suddenly not have that was difficult." Another participant, summing up what she felt she had learned from the turnoff, commented, "I was surprised to find out that even after three months, when I was really tired but didn't want to sleep, I still gravitated toward the television. My brain seems to be wired to think that TV is the easy escape from mental processing."

And for good reason: TV *is* an easy means to escape. The power of an addiction to anaesthetize, to tamp down unwanted thoughts and emotions and conjure up a sense of well-being, goes a long way toward explaining its appeal. Once the addiction is broken, however, feelings that we might prefer to suppress tend to rise up and begin clamoring for attention. At least for Cheryl, this process—although by no means easy—had its rewards. "I started dealing with some of my emotions because I couldn't numb myself anymore," she wrote. "There were a couple of days when I really could have used some TV! I definitely had time to think more, and I've taken care of some personal issues that have been ignored for a long time. Overall, that was a good thing, but the process was rough at times." Learning to live with ourselves—to acknowledge and respond to feelings that addiction kept at bay—can be challenging, even painful. It helps to bear in mind that an upsurge of emotions is a natural part of the coming alive that takes place once an addiction is lifted and that dealing with our feelings, rather than trying to ignore them, is almost certain to result in greater emotional maturity and balance.

Partly because addiction does so often function as a coping mechanism, recovering addicts sometimes discover that they have relinquished their primary addiction only to substitute another, at least in the short run. As Mike's experience suggests, recovering TV addicts are no exception. "I did replace watching TV with surfing the Internet for news," he admitted. "It became my new escape. But I don't think it was as bad a habit as TV. It didn't occupy as much time." Fortunately, as recovering addicts of all sorts can attest, more often than not replacement addictions turn out to be less compelling and less harmful and, over time, can simply fall away of their own accord.

One young mother confessed that at one point during the three months she got sick and used the TV as a babysitter for her two- and six-year-olds "instead of exerting the energy needed to chase them around the house and referee bouts of sibling rivalry." Having myself wished on occasion that the electronic babysitter were an option, I can sympathize with her predicament. One of the advantages of being a TV-free "old-timer" is that you eventually build up a repertoire of alternatives to TV. But this does take time. Especially in the early stages, those attempting to adjust to life without television may rue the loss of certain pleasures or rituals for which television provided the occasion. As another mother reported, "I have a very wiggly two-year-old, and one of my favorite morning activities had been to cuddle up in the rocking chair with her. While she was glued to *Teletubbies* or *Barney*, she forgot she wasn't wiggling and would actually sit still and snuggle with me. Without the diversion of the TV she won't sit still in my lap, and I miss that. We read, but she won't snuggle while reading—she wiggles."

Such losses are very genuine and may simply need to be mourned, although attempting to put them in perspective can also be a valuable strategy. If, for instance, the only way a two-year-old can be persuaded not to wiggle is by setting her in front of a television set, then is the "snuggle time" really worth the price being paid? One of the TV-free mothers who responded to my original survey confessed that on cold, wet, dreary days, she sometimes has second thoughts about not owning a TV. "About two or three times a year," she wrote, "especially in February when the weather has kept us cooped up for days, I fleetingly wish for a TV to give me an hour's break in the middle of the afternoon. That feeling usually passes, however, when I pick an armload of good books from the shelves and snuggle in with our three children for a grand reading session. Makes me glad my wish didn't come true!" Trite though it may seem, reflecting on the benefits to be had from not watching television—focusing on the gains rather than the losses—can help ease the pain of withdrawal.

Quite apart from personal losses of one sort or another, one factor that inevitably complicates the pursuit of a TV-free existence is the fact that our culture is so thoroughly saturated with television. Other than in the privacy of one's own home, it can be astonishingly difficult to get away from TV. In my view, establishing a TV-free household is already a major accomplishment, and it is generally sufficient to bring about significant change. Attempting to go further—vowing never to lay eyes on television—seems to me unwarranted and, where children are concerned, possibly even counterproductive: the "forbidden fruit" syndrome will only heighten TV's allure when kids find themselves away from home. All the same, the newly TV free are in a situation similar to that of an alcoholic in the early stages of recovery, who must find a way to live in a world where a majority of people still drink. "One thing I've really noticed is that when someone turns on a TV, I'm instantly drawn to it," one participant observed. "Even if I don't want to watch it, it demands my attention. I just have to walk away or I'll get sucked into it once again." Another woman confessed that she had fallen briefly off the wagon in the company of an old friend, who wanted to watch TV. "But the show I watched was really horrible," she added, "and it reaffirmed my commitment to being TV free." By way of explanation, this woman said she felt it would have been rude for her to refuse to join her friend in front of the television. Possibly so. Then again, provided she was willing to state a preference, perhaps it was rude of her friend not to respect her desire to do something other than watch TV.

As we saw in chapter 5, the TV-free decision can make others uncomfortable, usually because they sense (whether rightly or wrongly) a veiled criticism of their own TV-prone habits. Among the revelations listed by the young woman who wrote in at the end of the second month was: "The surprisingly negative reaction from friends!" She went on to comment that "since my boyfriend has given up TV, his friends are concerned that I might be brainwashing him. How ironic!" Another participant mentioned that she was being careful not to tell too many of her acquaintances that she was involved in the Cold-Turkey Turnoff "because people tend to get defensive." Then she shared this anecdote: "When I told a teacher at the elementary school that I'm working at, her reply was representative of the other people I've told. She said something like, 'Oh, I don't watch that much TV. I just put the news on in the morning when

I'm getting ready, maybe *Oprah* in the afternoon, the news around din-nertime, and only one or two shows in the evening, but not sitcoms or anything—*Dateline* or something like that.'" In the face of defensive or even hostile reactions, a sense of humor can definitely be a godsend. It can also be useful to remember that if others feel threatened by your choice of lifestyle, chances are the problem is theirs, not yours.

That said, TV-free individuals are likely at times to feel, or be made to feel, as if they are social misfits. "One of the most interesting things about this experience has been the incredulity of friends and acquain-tances whom we've told about going without television," wrote Sally, of Sally and Rob. "You'd think we had decided to go live on the moon or something. I guess this shows how much television has become in-grained, taken for granted." In reply to one of the questions put to partic-ipants at the end of the three months, about the negative aspects of their experience, Sally also observed, with some amusement: "I feel the only negative aspect is that future small talk with some folks in the USA is going to change! It is truly amazing how many people spend most of their time together talking about television programs and commercials. People will think I am a little strange because, when I have kids, I'm not plopping them in front of a TV for hours on end instead of playing with them!" Sally's reaction was shared by participants in my earlier survey, many of whom commented that abstaining from TV left them out of step with the mainstream. As one of them put it, "I don't feel less well informed, but I do feel that I know less trivia, less popular culture, and recognize fewer personalities from areas that receive a lot of TV atten-tion, such as music and the world of so-called Hollywood stars. This is not a problem for me, but I think it does require a strong sense of self to be content with being different."

Giving up an addiction is never easy, particularly when the addiction is so commonplace as to be regarded as normal. Successfully kicking the TV habit requires not only a genuine desire to try out a new way of living but the willingness and fortitude to persevere long enough to get over the initial period of withdrawal. "I think the first two weeks of going TV free are the hardest," wrote one of the participants in the turnoff. "It's just like any other habit or addiction: it takes some work to change these pat-

living outside the box

terns." At the same time, another offered the following analogy. Let's say we have a nice, big desk, with a lamp, a few framed photographs, pens and notepads, a plant, and a small TV set. The TV breaks, and so we take it away to be fixed. While it's gone, do we sit and stare at the empty spot on the desk? No, we fill it with new things—a vase of flowers, a small puzzle to play with, a diary, another photo. Then the TV set reappears, and we realize we're going to have to get rid of things in order to create space for it. But what to let go of? It may just be that there's no room for the TV now—that we've grown too fond of the new items, which have come to mean more to us than the TV did.

Some Words of Advice   When participants were asked, at the close of the three months, whether they intended to remain TV free, 30 percent answered yes. Another 60 percent said they planned to cut back on their viewing significantly, while 10 percent felt that their TV habits would remain unchanged. Every single participant, however—even those who were not able to remain TV free for the entire three months—said the experiment was worthwhile. Nearly three-quarters of the participants claimed that their physical fitness and their relationships with family members had improved, half noticed a positive change in their mental outlook, and 60 percent said they had discovered new pastimes or developed new hobbies (or both).

On the basis of their experience, participants in the turnoff had a number of helpful hints to offer those who are contemplating giving up TV. One said that going cold turkey was probably the best approach. "It's hard to cut back partially because you still see commercials for all the shows you're missing, and then you think you have to see them," he pointed out. "Make sure you have an outlet," Karen advised. "If you don't have a hobby, you will definitely want to look into finding one because you are going to have lots of time on your hands." "I found that it was important to tell people that I wasn't watching television," Jason reported. "Usually people would turn off the television when I was in the room if they knew that I couldn't watch. I also found it very helpful to build a community of people to do things with who didn't watch television. For instance, I found a running partner who trained with me five or six days a week, and I found a climbing partner to go to the climbing gym with me two or three times a week." Karen also felt that support from others was crucial to success. "I couldn't have quit if my husband was watching TV every evening," she commented.

Another participant—the mother of two small children—likewise emphasized the importance of shared activities. "It doesn't take a rocket scientist to figure out that families are a lot healthier when they play together more," she wrote. "Kids are kinesthetic by nature and need to learn about the world through tactile experiences. Get rid of the tube and go play on the swings or toss a Frisbee around. We joined an athletic club and signed the whole family up for swim classes. It's a great bonding experience for my husband and my two-year-old daughter to do the parent-tot swim class together." She added that her six-year-old had recently set himself the goal of trying out for the swim team, from which he had already begun to benefit: "Because he wants to be on the swim team he now asks me to remind him he doesn't want to eat junk food and candy because he wants to be healthy, so when he gets on the swim team he can be the best swimmer he can be."

Above all, the survivors said, hang in there. "Don't give up within the first month of no TV," was Karen's advice to anyone trying to kick the habit. "That is a hard time. But after that month, you'll soon discover that you don't miss the TV and that you value your new free time more." No doubt there will be moments when television, with its promise of instant relaxation (or mental oblivion), will seem like a mighty good thing. But TV addicts take heart: the habit *can* be broken. Hundreds of TV-free individuals and families across the country are living proof.

living outside the box

9: voices of experience

I say "go for it." You already know it's the right thing to do. So go ahead and listen to that voice in the back of your head that says TV is junk and you're wasting your time on it.

—Kerry,
one of the participants in the Cold-Turkey Turnoff

Although still relatively new, the idea of challenging children and adults to try their hand at complete withdrawal from TV, whether for a relatively brief or a more extended period, is gaining momentum. Since 1995, over 24 million individuals—10 million in 2006 alone—have sampled life without TV by participating in National TV-Turnoff Week, sponsored each April by the Center for Screen-Time Awareness. Taking part in TV-Turnoff Week encourages people to discover the hundreds of other activities available as alternatives to television, the vast majority of which offer greater physical, emotional, and creative stimulation. Moreover, evidence suggests that even a one-week recess from television can have a permanent effect on heavy viewing habits.

By way of a follow-up to my original survey of TV-free individuals and families, I invited those who had participated to respond to a series of questions of the sort that someone contemplating the decision to give up television might ask. Some of their answers, and in particular some of the specific suggestions they had to offer, seem worth sharing.

Q: *I would like to eliminate television or at least cut back significantly on my viewing, but I worry I will lose touch with world and local news. How do TV-free families keep up?*

Many of my respondents reported that listening to National Public Radio in the morning and evening, coupled with reading the local newspaper, kept them both informed and involved—well able to keep up with anyone else in discussions of the news. Several also mentioned checking the Internet headlines as an excellent way to stay on top of newsworthy developments. In addition, a large number indicated that they regularly read magazines such as *Time, Newsweek,* or the *Atlantic Monthly*—publications that offer broad coverage and relatively in-depth analysis. As a result, a great many felt that they were actually better informed than those who rely solely on television as their source of information. One commented: "When I watch TV news (particularly local news), I am invariably struck by how poor it is." Quite a few also complained of television's tendency to focus on sensationalistic stories and images. "TV tries to capture your emotions," wrote one couple. "The newspaper gives you the facts, some pictures, and some commentary on the events." Or as a woman from Houston, who said she relied on the newspaper and the Internet, put it: "I am fully informed and not hysterical."

Q: *I often sit down to watch one special favorite show, then end up—fours hours later—turning the TV off and going to bed. What happened!? Any advice?*

One woman offered this idea: "Set the kitchen timer or an alarm clock for the time your special show ends, and when the buzzer goes off, get up and turn off the TV. You could also have a friend call you at the time the program ends, and then you could turn off the TV for a little chat." Similarly, a TV-free family from Michigan suggested, "Make plans for something right at the time the show is ending, and always give priority to people, books, and activities over TV—even your favorite show!" A single dad from California proposed yet another approach: "Record that special show so that you can watch it later, at a convenient time. Don't let yourself check what's on the TV when you play your tape, and fast-forward through the commercials. What you may find is that you have better things to do than watch the tape."

living outside the box

Q: If I get rid of the TV, will I end up spending more money on other enter-tainment?

The consensus here was a firm "No." As one remarked, "You will save money on all the things you don't need but buy anyway because they're so heavily advertised." "Don't see why," wrote another. "Why do people have this notion they need to be entertained? *Do* something—make a quilt, play the piano, read a book, write a book, build an airplane, paint a picture." Others took into account what they saved by not subscribing to cable or by not having to replace aging TV sets. And, as one woman pointed out, ""Knowing my friends and family and sharing life with them doesn't cost anything."

One TV-free couple, who are the parents of young children, said they keep a small table covered with books, Legos, and puzzles. In addition, one of the drawers in the kitchen is strictly devoted to writing materials (including envelopes and stamps), and each of their children has a small bin of art supplies stocked with markers, glue, scissors, crayons, stickers, paper, and anything that will lend itself to a child's creativity. These parents said that the cost of all this was negligible compared to the expense of maintaining a TV and cable service, to say nothing of what it would cost to buy all the commercial products the kids would no doubt want. And, they said, the children's artwork provides them with an endless supply of great wall decorations.

Q: I would get rid of the TV, but my husband likes to veg out after a hard day at work and insists on several hours of TV each night. What to do?

A woman from Wisconsin had this advice to offer: "Set the example and get involved. Read, get out of the house and visit friends, go to concerts, sporting events, or volunteer for community service projects. Take walks, invite friends over, have regularly scheduled events in your family room. Be creative about how you spend your time. Your husband may never enjoy the quality of life that you'll discover without TV, but certainly do not wait for him to turn it off. Give him a reason to turn it off by your example and nothing more. Set the tone!" Her advice was seconded by a number of others, including her husband. "If you don't have children, leave the house, meet friends, join groups," he wrote. "In other words, let him come to you, instead of you coming to him and the TV."

Several others favored a more direct approach. "Distract that man!" one wife replied. "Invest in lingerie, read to him, buy a game to play together, find a hobby you can do together." Or women whose husbands are addicted to TV could try out this idea (suggested, not surprisingly, by a man): "Next time your husband sits down on the couch to veg out, put on a feathered negligee, curl up next to him, and purr!"

Q: *I'm a married man with children, but I'm addicted to sports and can't imagine Sundays without football. Can I get rid of my TV and still keep up?*

"Develop a strong loyalty to teams from Boston," was one TV-free dad's suggestion. "After a few years of heartbreak, it's easier to walk away from the tube." Then he added: "Seriously, I enjoy Sunday football, and for big games I sometimes go to a neighbor's house or maybe a sports bar." Another TV-free dad, who was equally a sports fanatic, commented, "If you really want to know what's going on in a game, listen to it on the radio. You won't be distracted by the players scratching their jocks or the fans throwing beer bottles." He said that he usually uses headphones to listen to the big games, which allows him to work outside in the yard or in his shop, where he can yell (or swear) to his heart's content while at the same time getting something done on a project.

Quite a few TV-free sports fans pointed out that if you listen to games on the radio, read the sports section in the paper or the sports news on the Internet, and attend professional sporting events when you can, you'll know as much if not more than TV-watching fans. Better yet, they argued, start *doing* sports, rather than watching them. "Join a local sports program, get out of the house, and play the game you love," one suggested. "Tag football is fun, and you might make a few new friends." "Don't watch life—live it," urged another. "You'll find you miss the TV less each day, and you'll feel healthier and more energetic, too."

Q: *I would like to get rid of the TV, but I worry I'll miss out on what everyone's talking about or be teased for not keeping up with popular shows. What can I expect?*

"The chance to be an individual!" was one reply. "Water off a duck's back!" declared a woman from Atlanta. "You can be thankful they make fun of you about such a stupid thing. Tell them to get a life! If you were bored and unimaginative, you'd spend your time watching TV, too." "You will never miss a thing!" another answered. "And once you move off TV, people will find you much more interesting because you will have so much more to offer." A family from California had a similar response: "When you stop watching TV, you'll find you have more time to do other, more meaningful things. You can explore interests and talents. After a while, you'll be amazed at the shallowness of the shows your peers find so important." One young man, who had been raised without television, called attention to a reaction we've already encountered. "Believe it or not," he reported, "a lot of the responses I've had in the past regarding growing up without a TV didn't consist of teasing but were almost defensive: 'Well, I only watch it for the news and stuff.' And I've never worried too much about who just got kicked off the island in *Survivor II*."

But if adults can generally laugh off the reactions of others, children often have a harder time of it, and parents may need to help them out. "My kids have been teased from time to time about being out of it, for not knowing what happened on this show or that show last night, or not even knowing who this character or that character is, and this bothers one of them more than the other," a single mother from California replied. "I think it does contribute to making them feel different, and that is not always fun for kids, but I don't see them being scarred by it." Moreover, as the mother from Atlanta pointed out, "Kids can find and cultivate friends who share their interests rather than feeling pressured to conform to a norm. Parents have a role here in influencing their kids' ability to judge the choices of their peers." Another family reported that "no one believed our kids" when they said they didn't have a TV. "Other kids were somewhat in awe of them, as it was out of their realm of possibility to imagine life without a TV. As far as 'missing out,' most TV shows are inane enough that our kids never had to listen very long before they'd figured out the whole thing."

Q: *We'd like to do other things, but a few hours of TV each evening has simply become a habit over the years. How can we get our evenings back?*

"The first step to me would be finding replacement activities that you enjoy," one TV-free father replied. "If you enjoy the news, read newspapers instead of getting it from the television. If you enjoy movies, get DVDs instead, and limit the number of movies you watch. If you enjoy comedy or sitcoms, try going to live comedy shows occasionally. In my family, I often read to the kids or go for bike rides with them." Another couple seconded his approach: "Find something that you always dreamed of doing, like going back to school or writing poetry, and then turn off the TV and do it. The joy you find in pursuing your dream will help you break the TV habit."

"Rearrange the furniture, move the TV to the basement and don't have it where you sit to relax," was the suggestion of one TV-free family. "Have furniture grouped for conversation instead of all aimed at the TV. Put the TV in a cabinet and keep the doors *shut*. If you don't see it, you won't automatically think of turning it on." One couple shared another idea: "Keep a log of what you watch and evaluate it after a week. Do you even remember those shows? Were they worth it? Buy some games and play them as a family. Investigate hobbies." Their advice was not unlike that of another couple: "Add up the amount of time that you spend with the TV in a month. Think about what you could accomplish if you devoted even a quarter of that time to something important (PTA, for example), and then make a commitment to something. Or just go to bed a little earlier and get a decent night's sleep!"

"Stock up on good books," one woman advised. "Don't be afraid to go outside, buy a star chart or telescope, plant a garden, join a club, go bowling! Dress up. Get to know your community, learn its history, and find hobbies." A Wisconsin family was full of ideas: "Go through the phone book under clubs, associations, and organizations, and find community groups that you might be interested in joining. Contact local bookstores about events and book clubs. Check out volunteer opportunities at church or get involved in community service projects. Get out of the house if you can. Use the time to take a walk or make a trip to the gym—or, if for some reason it's hard for you to get out, cultivate a hobby that you can pursue at home, like family genealogy. Or take that evening time to call friends and family, to invite people over, or just to read a book, magazine, or newspaper. If you have children, use the time to play games, ride bikes, take walks, go to the park, take on a family project, or read together out loud."

Reading aloud is indeed a lovely family activity. A New Hampshire father commented: "I need time with good books or some other relaxing activity, such as playing music, each evening in order to relax after work. My family has built up quite a selection of books we reread a lot, including some young-adult and so-called children's books. (Harry Potter books are of interest to many more people than just children.) We try to find new ones as well. When I was growing up, I remember my mother sitting on the sofa and reading while the rest of my family was watching TV. This was a relaxing activity for her, more so than the tube." One family started at the dinner table, with a book of jokes from the library. This led to printing funny quotes or stories off the Internet to read—anything that would get people laughing, joking, and talking. A Georgia family brought home a variety of good books on tape from the library. As one of the tapes began to play, the family would congregate in the living room. Choose a book with long chapters, they suggested, make sure there are comfortable places to sit and relax, and then play an hour or two of the tape each night. One mother had developed a similar ritual. Every evening, after she has made dinner, she reads a chapter from an exciting book aloud while the rest of the family cleans up the kitchen. Even her fourteen-year-old son hates to miss out, she reported.

Q: *I am a parent with two small toddlers. I'd like to give the TV-free life a try, but how will I be able to get anything done without using videos as a babysitter for a few hours each day?*

Many of my respondents pointed out that kids have a natural ability to entertain themselves and merely have to be provided with alternatives to sitting in front of the TV. Several suggested equipping children with art supplies or other projects to work on, as well as toys or books on tape. "If the kids don't have the option of TV, they will find other things to do," wrote one mother. "Your job is to make sure there is a stimulating environment." Another parent made a similar observation: "Kids will always find ways to amuse themselves. But if the TV is always there, they simply don't cultivate this skill." Another said that her children (aged three, six, and eight) are "content to sit and read independently for up to an hour at a time, just as my neighbors' kids watch TV." One TV-free dad said that he had placed a nice big set of maple building blocks in the family room right where the TV used to be. This guaranteed his children hours of fun, plenty of interaction, and experience with problem solving, as well as pride in an accomplishment. Several parents also pointed out that even quite small children can be taught to lend a hand with chores. "Have the toddlers help you," one couple proposed. "They learn fast and will soon be more of a help than a hindrance. When they're older, they can take over many of the chores you teach them now. Our four-year-old can take dishes out of the dishwasher, pick up toys, pick tomatoes, unpack groceries, fill the dry cat food dispenser, and fetch tools for a parent on a ladder."

Many TV-free parents also called attention to the question of priorities. Childhood passes by so quickly, they argued, so why not spend time with your children while you can, even if it means you don't get as much done around the house? "A few hours of reading library picture books or building block towers became a more worthy goal that dusting, vacuuming, making fancy meals, or having an immaculate yard," was one mother's comment. "Remember that toddlers don't last forever," wrote another, "and that the habits they form now, especially with regard to self-entertainment, will last a lifetime."

Q: *We little kids wish our parents would pay more attention to us instead of having family life revolve around the news and TV shows. How can we convince them to turn the TV off?*

One TV-free mom suggested, "Ask them to rearrange the furniture so that it's set up for conversation rather than for watching TV. Set up times with them (written schedules are good because grown-ups often say 'Later,' and then it never happens!) to do fun things. Playing card games, going for walks, having tea with friends, cooking—lots of simple things can add up to fun times with adults." "Challenge your parents to one night without TV," advised a dad from Wisconsin, "and encourage them to play games with you, to take you to the park for a little exercise, or to take a class at the YMCA with you. Get them to do this one day a week at first, and then the challenge is to add another day, and so on." His advice was seconded by another TV-free family: "Find things to do and then request that you do them. Once your parents see that you have a passion, they may follow your interests, and so even though you are kids, you can set the example. Also, make sure that, during those times not scheduled for TV, you ask your parents to read books aloud to you or to play games with you. Once your parents see that the time you spend together is meaningful and fun, they may just forget all about the TV shows. Request walks and family bike rides!"

I also heard from several children in connection with this question. "Tell them that they will be bad parents if they keep watching TV," suggested ten-year-old Tim. His six-year-old sister, Analisa, followed up with this advice: "There is really bad stuff on the TV and gross. Tell them that you will throw up if you have to watch it."

Q: *My daughter is home alone from about 3:30 until 6:00 p.m., and TV is her constant companion. Any suggestions for alternative ideas?*

"Throw out the TV," was the reaction of one mother. "If she is young enough to be worried about being home alone, get story tapes from the library. They do very different things as far as the imagination goes— the need to imagine the pictures sparks the brain, and it is possible to draw or do other things while listening." A father from Wisconsin offered a series of possibilities: "Leave her a list of tasks to be completed by the time you get home. Arrange an after-school activity for her. Engage her in a hobby that she can work on until you get home. Let her invite a friend over. Get her involved in a community service project during that time, or in babysitting, or in after-school activities such as music lessons. . . . There are so many things to do!" Similarly, a family from Illinois suggested: "Give her tap-dancing lessons or a sports activity at the YMCA for her afternoons instead of TV. Making friends and having fun with others will be more beneficial to your daughter than being alone at home with the TV." Moreover, as a couple from Indiana pointed out, "If a child is old enough to be home alone for two and a half hours, she is old enough to sit with a lonely neighbor, a harried young mother, or a handicapped friend and learn to be of assistance."

Q: *My kids are in high school and grew up with plenty of TV. They are good kids. Could we still benefit by turning off the TV, or is it too late?*

The overwhelming consensus was, of course, that it's never too late. As one woman put it: "You can always reap the benefit of living a fuller life!" Another woman, who said that she had been weaned on the TV in its early days, back in the fifties, agreed. "I was forty-five when I turned off the TV and haven't regretted it for one moment," she declared. "If they still watch a lot, yes," wrote a mother from California. "I believe that one reason my children are relatively free thinkers is their lack of exposure to the kinds of societal pressure shown on TV—the too-thin women, the stereotypes in commercials and programs, and so on. During the teen years these pressures are especially strong." In the words of another mother: "It's never too late. You owe it to them to turn it off so that you can get involved with each other—time is running out. As teens, they still need to learn household skills and have conversations. Turning off the TV can afford you some time to catch up. It won't be a piece of cake, but your kids are worth it!"

"They can still benefit," was the opinion of ten-year-old Tim. "They wouldn't see trash, and they could get more exercise and read." A TV-free father from Indiana summed it up: "Every TV hour is taken from doing something else. It is never too late to learn that we have to set priorities in life. We can never reclaim time or save it up. Ask yourself, 'Is what I'm doing really worth the time I am giving it?'"

Q: *I've been thinking of using TV as a reward or taking TV away as a punishment with my kids. Would I be sending the wrong message?*

The resounding response was "Yes!" As one mother put it: "If you want TV to be the most important thing in their lives, use it as a reward." A number of TV-free parents suggested that some sort of shared family activity was a far better approach to rewarding children. "Hug them and tell them you love them, and then do something together," wrote one mother, while another proposed, "Why don't you use a trip to the bookstore or a family bike ride as a reward?" Praise them, spend time with them, let them do something they've been asking to do—but, whatever else, leave TV out of the reward-and-punishment realm.

Q: *We want to quit watching TV, but should we go cold turkey or cut back gradually?*

Most of those who responded to this question recommended the cold-turkey approach. "Seems easier to just quit and be done with it," said one. "After three weeks, I no longer wanted TV. But those three weeks are the toughest. Get out of the house, change your routine, and reward yourself with something at the end of each week. Remember, it's not easy changing a habit. Just be sure you replace it with something constructive." Or, as another proposed: "Just turn it off and keep a journal. You'll see the benefits in a matter of days!"

"Cold turkey is truly the best way," said another. "Fill the time with other activities. Read, play games, develop a hobby, or listen to music. If you decide to cut back gradually, choose your favorite programs and record them. You'll save time by fast-forwarding through the commercials, and you'll probably discover that you find other things to do and don't even watch everything you've taped." "Go cold turkey," urged yet another. "You owe it to yourself and to your kids. Enjoy each other. After all, there must be some reason why you live together. Maybe you like each other?"

Q: *What are the greatest trials and the greatest benefits of life without TV?*

Not surprisingly, my respondents had more to say about the benefits of the TV-free life than about its trials. "Every now and then there is a show I'd like to watch (usually a special on something interesting), and it's too much trouble to find a friend who can tape it," replied one woman. "But there are so many things in life I take great interest in, so it's not a big deal." Another mentioned, with obvious amusement, the sometimes incredulous reaction of other people: "Occasionally, I am greeted with disbelief—*'You don't watch TV???'* And that isn't much of a trial!" Another proposed that "not being very good at trivia games" was the greatest drawback.

And the greatest benefits? A few pointed to specific accomplishments, such as finishing a college degree; others mentioned freedom from incessant advertising or from the constant noise of the TV set. But the resounding response was "Time." Time to talk with family and friends, time to play, to read, to reflect, to put your feet up and unwind. Time to learn, to create, to pursue a hobby, to get involved with the community. Time to do whatever you enjoy doing, rather than trying to squeeze life in between TV shows. One comment speaks for all: "I have much more time than I used to, and every moment is filled with things I choose to do."

10: time for reflection

Dost thou love life? Then squander not time, for that is the stuff life is made of.
—**Benjamin Franklin**

My working title for this book was "No TV? No Big Deal!" In other words, in the eyes of TV-free families, life without television is perfectly natural. They no longer think about the decision, nor do they generally feel any particular need to justify their choice to others. The issue is moot: they know that getting rid of the TV was a good move. The more I thought about it, however, the more I realized that living without television is actually a very big deal. Again and again, TV-free parents claimed that eliminating TV from the household was the best parenting decision they ever made and that their own lives had become richer and more rewarding as a result. Choosing to turn off the TV had also provided them with some relief from the white noise that surrounds us. They had discovered that the silence between the drumbeats is as important as the sound of the drum.

Attempting to convince the population at large of the value of the "off" button may seem a fool's errand. But I am a firm believer in Margaret Mead's words: "Never doubt that a small group of thoughtful, committed citizens can change the world." I also have little doubt what the future might look like if we do nothing about screen time in America. We are already on overload. America may be the most productive nation in the world, but that is not because we work more efficiently and with greater concentration. Rather, it is because we put in more hours on the job. Approximately 80 percent of American men and 62 percent of women now work more than forty hours a week.[1] We are, moreover, held hostage by the technology we have created—which, among other things means that our workplace can follow us home. "Today, the constant ping-ing of your e-mail can be like the drip-drip-drip of water torture. We're swimming in doodads and options—text messaging and search engines, Blackberries and blogs, Wi-fi, cell phones that try to do all of the above, and the promise that we haven't seen anything yet."[2] It's easy to see how good leisure gets lost in the shuffle.

We are also inundated with information, whether we want it or not. The television news has become a three-ring circus, what with one or two main items in the middle of the screen and banner headlines streaming across the bottom. We can Google up just about anything in a matter of seconds, often without pausing to consider whether the information we have just retrieved is reliable. In fact, educators have begun to worry about what all this instant access to knowledge is doing to our capacity for crit-ical thought. As Bill McKibben, author of *Enough: Staying Human in an Engineered Age*, points out, "There's the real danger that one is absorbing and responding to bursts of information, rather than having time to think"—the danger of "having so many trees that there's no possibility of seeing the forest." Similarly, in the opinion of Professor David Levy, of the University of Washington's Information School, "We're losing touch with the contemplative roots of scholarship, the reflective dimension."[3] In 2004, Levy—who makes a point of taking a one-day holiday from tech-nology each week—organized a conference called "Information, Silence, and Sanctuary," with a view to focusing attention on our need to slow down and make room for our thoughts.

In an increasingly frantic effort to keep up with our lives, we are also multitasking like madmen, despite the fact that attempting to do two or three things at once is very often counterproductive, sometimes risky, and just plain exhausting. We wind up suffering from cognitive overload, to the point that, by the time we get home at night, we're so stressed that all we want to do is turn on the TV and collapse. The irony, of course, is that zoning out in front of the TV does not actually leave us refreshed. As we have learned, watching TV is an essentially counterfeit form of relax-ation. We are, for one thing, confronted with a veritable kaleidoscope of sounds and images, many of which are urging us to buy something. More to the point, we are not processing anything while we are sitting in

living outside the box

front a TV screen. We are not sorting through the day's experiences or getting in touch with our emotional state of being or using our minds to create or build or play. We are not genuinely recuperating.

We are also choosing to isolate ourselves. Reams have been written about the death of community in America, about social disconnection, about the spiritual vacuum in our lives. The problem, in all its manifestations and complexities, has been identified and thoroughly well described. But what about the solution? Complex social ailments seldom (if ever) have a single, simple cure. Nonetheless, one part of the remedy seems all but self-evident. "People who say that TV is their 'primary form of entertainment' volunteer and work on community projects less often, attend fewer dinner parties and fewer club meetings, spend less time visiting friends, entertain at home less, picnic less, are less interested in politics, give blood less often, write friends less, regularly, make fewer long-distance calls, send fewer greeting cards and less e-mail, and express more road rage than demographically matched people who differ only in saying that TV is *not* their primary form of entertainment," writes Robert Putnam in *Bowling Alone*.[4] It stands to reason, then, that if we wish to reconnect, turning off the TV would be a good place to start.

If nothing else, I hope that reading this book has convinced you of one thing, namely, that life without television is far worse in the anticipation than the event. As those who have embarked on the journey can (and do) attest, the initial disorientation, the sense of sudden loss, quickly gives way to a process of discovery, in which new pleasures and new pursuits open up. Listen to TV-free individuals, and they will tell you: it is living *inside* the box that entails the loss. But in order to make this discovery, you do have to take that first step.

Anyone interested in giving life without TV a try should make a point of visiting the Web site of the Center for Screen-Time Awareness, formerly the TV-Turnoff Network: www.screentime.org (or www.tvturnoff.org). The TV-Turnoff Network was founded in 1994 with the goal of helping people understand that they have power over the place that television occupies in their lives. Since 1995, National TV-Turnoff Week has drawn upwards of 24 million participants. It is endorsed by more than seventy national organizations, including the American Medical Association, the American Academy of Pediatrics, and the President's Council on Physical Fitness, and has the support of thousands of schools, clubs, community groups, and religious congregations, which together organize the event at a local level. An Organizer's Kit is available for anyone who wishes to make TV-Turnoff Week happen in their area.

Follow-up surveys have indicated that a significant proportion of those who take part in TV-Turnoff Week wind up reducing their TV viewing over the long term. A plan adopted in 2007 encourages individuals and families to extend their commitment to reducing the amount of screen time in their lives by choosing to go Gold, Silver, or Bronze. Participants at all three levels must limit their screen time to a maximum of two hours a day on weekends (Friday evening to Sunday afternoon). To qualify for a Bronze, viewers must restrict their recreational screen use to no more than two hours a day on weekdays; for a Silver, they must limit themselves to no more than one hour a day. Those who cut out screen time altogether during the week have earned a Gold. If you would like to assert your independence from the tyranny of the TV but don't feel up to going cold turkey, you might consider adopting this approach.

In addition, the Center for Screen-Time Awareness has developed a program for use in elementary schools, "More Reading, Less TV," which is designed to improve students' reading habits and to foster a more positive attitude toward reading. Over 30,000 students have taken part in the program, and their reports have been overwhelmingly supportive. In particular, students who initially identify themselves as poor readers seem to gain substantially more confidence in their skills and are far more likely to seek out a book after the "More Reading, Less TV" program than before. In tandem with the American Academy of Pediatrics, the center has also launched a project called "America Live!" that offers families practical advice on how to reduce TV viewing. Much of that advice is contained in a publication titled *Turn It Off: Real Tips from Real Parents to Limit TV* that is available for download at no charge. As the project recognizes, abiding by the recommendations of pediatricians and other professionals is not always an easy matter for parents who are struggling to balance childrearing with jobs and household responsibilities. America Live! aims to help families find workable ways to cut back on TV. The center's Web site offers a wealth of other resources, including fact sheets, an online activity guide, and a list of 101 screen-free activities, as well as press releases, informational pages such as "Turn Off TV, Turn On a Healthier Lifestyle" and "Less TV Opens Doors to Literacy," links to important items of research, and a message board.

One of the links provided by the Center for Screen-Time Awareness is to the Web site of the California Obesity Prevention Initiative, which has developed a TV- and screen-reduction plan designed for use by after-school programs and youth serving agencies. Called "Do More, Watch Less," the COPI plan is the result of a collaborative effort on the part of the Center for Weight and Health at the University of California at Berkeley, California Project LEAN (Leaders Encouraging Activity and Nutrition), the University of California at San Francisco, and the TV-Turnoff Network and is available for download at http://www.dhs.ca.gov/ps/cdic/copi/copiforms/tvtool.htm. The program, which consists of four sessions that can span anywhere from two and a half weeks to a month, is specifically geared to "tweens"—ten- to fourteen-year-olds. As a preliminary step, participants spend a few days tracking the amount of time they devote to watching TV, surfing the Web, playing video games, and so on. They are then challenged to cut out all screen-based activities for three full days and after that to limit their screen time to no more than two hours a day. In addition to providing instructions on how to implement the plan, "Do More, Watch Less" also contains a list of screen-free activities as well as a short but extremely informative essay, "TV Viewing and Children's Health: A Call to Action." Anyone—parents, teachers, members of community groups, even children—can undertake to persuade local schools or youth organizations to adopt the plan.

In short, the resources are out there, for those who wish to make use of them. One might also consider another approach to curtailing screen time and, more generally, restoring a measure of sanity to one's life. As we know, Barbara Kingsolver is already a card-carrying member of the TV-free population. But once every summer she goes a step further:

> I purposefully spend a few weeks each year avoiding national
> and international news altogether, and attending only to the

time for reflection   153 news of my own community, since that is the only place I can actually do very much about the falling-apart-things of the moment. Some of my friends can't believe I do this, or can't understand it. One summer I was talking on the phone with a friend when she derived from our conversation that I had not yet heard about the tragic crash of the small airplane piloted by John Kennedy Jr.

"You're *kidding!*" she cried, again and again. "It happened three days ago, and you haven't heard about it yet?"

I hadn't.

My friend was amazed and amused. "People in Turkestan already know about this," she said.

I could have observed that everybody in the world, Turkestanis included, already knows global warming is the most important news on every possible agenda—except here in the United States, where that info has been successfully suppressed. We know so very much about the trees, and miss the forest. I was talking with a friend, though, so I told her only that I was deeply sorry for the Kennedy family, to whom this tragedy belonged, but that it would make no real difference in my life.

It's not that I'm callous about the calamities suffered by famous people: they are heartaches, to be sure, but heartaches genuinely experienced only by their own friends and families. It seems somewhat voyeuristic, and also absurd, to expect that JFK Jr.'s death should change my life any more than a recent death in *my* family affected the Kennedys. The same is true of a great deal—maybe most—of the other bad news that pounds at our doors day and night. On the matter of individual tragic deaths, I believe that those in my own neighborhood are the ones I need to attend to first, by means of casseroles and whatever else I can offer. I also believe it's possible to be so overtaken and stupefied by the tragedies of the world that we don't have any time or energy left for those closer to home, the hurts we should take as our own.

living outside the box

Many view this opinion as quaint. Truly, I'm in awe of the news junkies who can watch three screens at once and maintain their up-to-the-minute data without plunging into despair or cynicism. But I have a different sort of brain. For me, knowing does not replace doing. I find I sometimes need time off from the world of things I can't do anything about so I may be granted (as the famous prayer says) the serenity to accept the things I cannot change, the courage to change the things I can, and the wisdom to know the difference.

So for the duration of every summer, when our family migrates to a farm in rural Virginia (the place whose antique wiring would short out at the very idea of TV), I gather books and read up, seeking background information on the likes of genetic engineering, biodiversity, the history of U.S. relations in the Middle East—drifts of event too large and slow to be called news. I still listen almost daily to radio news (the Kennedy crash must not have been among All the Things to be Considered), but I limit myself to one national newspaper per week, usually the Sunday edition of the *Washington Post*, which I can buy on Monday or Tuesday at our little town's bookstore. Here's a big secret I've discovered that I will share with you now: This strategy saves me the time of reading about the sports hero/politician/movie star whose shocking assault charge/affair/heart attack was huge breaking news in the middle of last week, because by Sunday he has already confessed/apologized/died. You'd be amazed how little time it takes to catch up, not on "all the news that's fit to print," as one news organ boasts, but on all I really needed to be a responsible citizen.

Of course, Kingsolver is talking here about taking a holiday from more than just television. But the idea of declaring a time out, of observing a modern-day Sabbath, is gaining ground. Among the recommendations of "Tech Tonic," a report issued by the Alliance for Childhood, was that one day a week be set aside as an "electronic entertainment–free zone."

And David Levy is by no means the only person who has chosen to mark the Jewish Sabbath by unplugging from the electronic universe—including, of course, the TV set. One day a week may be a small beginning, but, as the saying goes, "If nothing changes, nothing changes." That one day of rest could be a turning point.

So is saying farewell to television a big deal or not? Provided one is willing to give the TV-free life an honest try, probably not. As we have seen, over three-quarters of the children who took part in "30 Days Live" made it through an entire month without screen time of any sort, while participants in the Cold-Turkey Turnoff repeatedly commented that withdrawal from television had been easier than they expected. Similarly, the TV-free individuals who responded to my original survey often reported that the withdrawal period had not proved especially difficult: TV's grip on them was not as powerful as they had thought. Even when family and friends failed to support their decision, the changes that ensued were so dramatically positive that these individuals simply could not imagine returning to their previous pattern of TV use. An overwhelming majority said they had *never* regretted their decision. So perhaps switching off the set really is no big deal.

But turning the TV off can turn into a very big deal when the family starts playing together, the kids start getting along better, relationships grow a little deeper, schedules become more manageable and stress lessens, and all sorts of new interests and activities begin to blossom. At the end of one's days, who wouldn't wish for a little more time to share with children and loved ones? Or a little more time for pursuing personal interests? But there's no reason to wait until the end. If you make what may initially seem like the lonesome and scary decision to turn off your TV once and for all, the withdrawal symptoms of the first few weeks will soon pale in comparison to the pleasures of the world of good leisure. And as you reach each TV-free milestone—three days, three weeks, three months, three years, or even the rest of your life—you will have the satisfaction of knowing you woke up in time to experience life as a participant rather than a spectator.

living outside the box

appendix a:
the tv-free survey

This is the first time such research has been conducted with a large number of TV-free people, and I very much appreciate your taking precious time to give me facts and details about your family life and the individuals in your home. In preliminary correspondence, many of you have mentioned varying "levels" of TV-free existence. If you watch more than 6 hours of television or videos per week, please do not take this survey. Note also that those without children can skip questions #55 through #88. All information will remain completely anonymous unless you would like to mention your name in the three short essay questions at the end. Material from the essays may be published at a future date. As you know, your participation in this research is voluntary, and you may withdraw from this study at any time.

The survey is divided into six parts. **Part 1**: Demographics; **Part 2**: Family Lifestyle; **Part 3**: The Information Age; **Part 4**: A Kid's Life; **Part 5**: The Community; and **Part 6**: Your Stories, Values, and Dreams.

Part 1: Demographics

1. How many adults are in your home?　❑ 1　❑ 2　❑ 3 or more

2. How many children are in your home?　❑ 1　❑ 2　❑ 3　❑ 4　❑ 5 or more

3. How old are the children in your family? *(check all that apply)*

❑ Under 1　❑ 1–3　❑ 4–6　❑ 7–9　❑ 10–15　❑ 16–20　❑ No children

4. How old are the adults in your family? *(check all that apply)*

❑ 20–30　❑ 31–40　❑ 41–50　❑ 51–60　❑ 61–70　❑ 71 and over

5. Which of the following represents the highest level of education that the adults in your home have completed? *(check all that apply)*

❑ Some high school or less　❑ High school graduate　❑ Some college

❑ Associate's degree　❑ Bachelor's degree　❑ Master's degree

❑ Doctoral degree

6. With which of the following groups or group do you most identify?

☐ African American   ☐ Asian American or Pacific Islander

☐ Latino   ☐ Native American

☐ White   ☐ Other

☐ Prefer not to answer

7. What is your gender?   ☐ Male   ☐ Female

8. What is your current marital status?

☐ Married   ☐ Single, never married   ☐ Separated or divorced   ☐ Widowed

9. Have you ever been divorced?   ☐ No   ☐ Yes

10. How would you classify your family "job status":

☐ Couple: mom home, dad works

☐ Couple: dad home, mom works

☐ Couple: mom and dad both work full time

☐ Couple: mom and dad work, one or both part time

☐ Single: work full time

☐ Single: work part time

☐ Single: not working

☐ Single: retired

☐ Other

11. Which best describes your personal income(s) before taxes last year?

☐ Under $20,000   ☐ $80,000–$99,999

☐ $20,000–$39,999   ☐ $100,000–$129,000

☐ $40,000–$59,999   ☐ $130,000 or more

☐ $60,000–$79,999

12. Do the adults in your home have a savings and/or retirement plan?

☐ No   ☐ Yes

13. If you have a savings and/or retirement plan, approximately what percentage of your income(s) per year is designated to the plan?

☐ None ☐ 1%–3%   ☐ 4%–6 %   ☐ 7%–10%   ☐ 11%–15%   ☐ 16%–20% ☐ over 20%

14. Do your children have savings accounts?   ☐ No   ☐ Yes   ☐ No children

15. How would you classify your residence?   ☐ Urban   ☐ Suburban   ☐ Rural

16. Do you own or rent your home?   ☐ Own   ☐ Rent

17. In what type of home do you live?

☐ Apartment   ☐ House   ☐ Mobile home   ☐ Other

18. Do you have a religious affiliation?   ☐ No   ☐ Yes

19. If so, please indicate your faith or denomination (Jewish, Methodist, Catholic, Unitarian Universalist, etc.) or simply leave blank: _____

20. What kind of school do your children attend? *(check all that apply)*

❑ Public   ❑ Private   ❑ Home schooling

21. Please tell me what state you are from (use two capital letters): _____

Part 2: Family Lifestyle

(Please note: The term *family* is intended to represent your entire household, consisting of one or more persons.)

22. How many dinners do you sit down to as a family per week?

❑ 1 or none   ❑ 2–3   ❑ 4–5   ❑ 6–7

23. How long do you sit at the table for your average dinnertime?

❑ Less than 15 minutes   ❑ 15–30 minutes   ❑ 30–45 minutes   ❑ 45 minutes or more

24. How often do you eat out as a family per month (on average)?

❑ Never   ❑ 1 time   ❑ 2 times   ❑ 3 times   ❑ 4 or more times

25. If you have children, how often do you eat out without the kids per month?

❑ Never   ❑ 1 time   ❑ 2 times   ❑ 3 times   ❑ 4 or more times

26. How many minutes of "meaningful" conversation do you have with your child or children on a typical day? (Please write in numerals: 5, 24, etc.) _____

27. How many minutes of "meaningful" conversation do you have with your spouse or partner on a typical day? (If no spouse or partner, leave blank.) _____

28. OPTIONAL: This survey reveals a snapshot of your lifestyle and satisfaction. As sexual interaction is sometimes thought to be a measure of marital happiness, please state how many times per week you have sex with your spouse or partner:

❑ 0   ❑ 1   ❑ 2   ❑ 3   ❑ 4   ❑ 5 or more

29. Do you feel your marriage is stronger because of the lack of TV in your home?

❑ No   ❑ Yes   ❑ No difference   ❑ Not married

30. How would you describe your life at home?

❑ Always rushed   ❑ Often rushed   ❑ Sometimes rushed

❑ Rarely rushed   ❑ Never rushed

31. How much "downtime" (unplanned or free time) does your whole family experience *together* per day?

❑ Less than 15 minutes   ❑ 16–30 minutes   ❑ 31–60 minutes

❑ 1–2 hours   ❑ Over 2 hours

32. What are the various activities going on in your home during this downtime?

Activity: _____

Activity: _____

Activity: _____

33. About what percentage of this downtime does your family spend outdoors (other than in inclement weather)?

- ☐ 75% or more of our time
- ☐ About half of our time
- ☐ Less than 25% of our time
- ☐ Between 50% and 75% of our time
- ☐ Between 25% and 50% of our time

34. What is the most common "substitute activity" for TV in your family?

Activity: _____

35. What are the typical adult activities in your home between 9:00 and 11:00 p.m. or after the kids go to bed?

Activity: _____

Activity: _____

Activity: _____

36. If you have more than one child, how much time per day do your children spend playing or interacting *only with each other?*

- ☐ 1–14 minutes
- ☐ 15–29 minutes
- ☐ 30–59 minutes
- ☐ 1–2 hours
- ☐ 2–4 hours
- ☐ No children or only one child

37. Do you feel that your children get along better because there's no TV in your home?

- ☐ No   ☐ Yes   ☐ No difference   ☐ No children

38. How many outside social groups is the dad in your home involved in (on his own)?

- ☐ 0   ☐ 1   ☐ 2   ☐ 3   ☐ 4 or more   ☐ No dad in my home

39. Please mark the type of group or groups in which he is involved:

- ☐ Civic organization
- ☐ School related
- ☐ Other
- ☐ Sports or fitness related
- ☐ Church related
- ☐ No outside social groups
- ☐ Book related
- ☐ Hobby related
- ☐ No dad in my home

40. How many outside social groups is the mom involved in (on her own)?

- ☐ 0   ☐ 1   ☐ 2   ☐ 3   ☐ 4 or more   ☐ No mom in my home

41. Please mark the type of group or groups in which she is involved:

- ☐ Civic organization
- ☐ School related
- ☐ Other
- ☐ Sports or fitness related
- ☐ Church related
- ☐ No outside social groups
- ☐ Book related
- ☐ Hobby related
- ☐ No mom in my home

42. What type of pets (if any) do you have at your home? *(check all that apply)*
☐ Cat   ☐ Dog   ☐ Horse or other large animal   ☐ Small caged animal
☐ Other   ☐ No pets

43. Which of the following do you have at your home? *(check all that apply)*
☐ Recycling plan   ☐ Compost bin   ☐ Vegetable garden
☐ Herb garden   ☐ Animals for food production   ☐ None listed here

44. How many cars do you own?   ☐ 0   ☐ 1   ☐ 2   ☐ 3   ☐ 4 or more

45. Does anyone in your family ever ride-share, use other commuter options, or bicycle or walk to and from work?   ☐ No   ☐ Yes

Part 3: The Information Age

46. Some participants in this survey own a TV but watch only a very limited amount; others do not own a TV or watch TV or videos at all. What level of "TV free" are you?
☐ Do not own, rent, or borrow a TV at all and do not watch TV anywhere else
☐ Do not own, rent, or borrow a TV but occasionally watch TV at a friend's house
☐ Do not own a TV but rent or borrow occasionally for special movies or shows
☐ Own a TV but have set it up so that it plays only videos
☐ Own a TV, watch network very rarely (Olympics, major events, playoffs, etc.)
☐ Own a TV, watch a limited amount of network and cable
☐ Own a TV, watch a limited amount of cable only
☐ Other

47. Some families have made changes in their TV habits fairly recently. When would you say you either severely cut back or became TV free?
☐ Within the past 6 months   ☐ Within the past year   ☐ 1–3 years ago
☐ 4–6 years ago   ☐ 7–10 years ago   ☐ Over 10 years ago

48. How many hours of television do you watch per week (on average)?
☐ I watch none   ☐ Less than 30 minutes   ☐ 30–60 minutes
☐ 1–3 hours   ☐ 4–6 hours
☐ Over 6 hours *(Please discontinue this survey and watch for the results!)*

49. How often do you go to the movies in a typical month?
☐ Never   ☐ 1–2 times   ☐ 3–4 times   ☐ 5 or more times

50. How many library books do you check out per month?
☐ None   ☐ 1–5   ☐ 6–10   ☐ 11–15   ☐ 16–20   ☐ 21 or more

51. How many computers do you own?
☐ None   ☐ 1   ☐ 2   ☐ 3 or more

52. How many hours per week do the adults in your family use a home computer for enjoyment (that is, for other than work-related tasks)?

❏ Not at all ❏ 1–3 hours ❏ 4–6 hours ❏ 7–9 hours ❏ 10 hours or more

53. Do you feel the adults in your home use the computer too much? ❏ No ❏ Yes

54. Do you feel the computer has taken over the role of TV in your home?

❏ No ❏ Yes ❏ Not sure

Those with children, please answer questions #55 through #88; those without children may proceed to question #89. Thank you!

55. Does your child have a computer in his or her room? ❏ No ❏ Yes

56. Do your children play Nintendo and/or other computer games? ❏ No ❏ Yes

57. How many hours per week do your children spend playing Nintendo and/or other computer games?

❏ None ❏ Less than 1 hour ❏ 1–3 hours ❏ 4–6 hours ❏ 7–9 hours

❏ 10 hours or more

58. Do your children visit computer-based "chat rooms" with their friends?

❏ No ❏ Yes

59. How many hours per week do your children spend "chatting"?

❏ None ❏ 1–3 hours ❏ 4–6 hours ❏ 7–9 hours ❏ 10 hours or more

60. Do your children surf the net? ❏ No ❏ Yes

61. How many hours per week do your children spend surfing the net?

❏ They do not surf the net ❏ Less than 30 minutes ❏ 30 to 60 minutes

❏ 1–2 hours ❏ 3–4 hours ❏ 5–6 hours

❏ 7–9 hours ❏ 10 hours or more

62. Do you limit your children's use of the computer? ❏ No ❏ Yes

63. Do you feel your children use the computer too much? ❏ No ❏ Yes

Part 4: A Kid's Life

64. About how many hours per week (on average) are your children involved in physical activity?

❏ Less than 60 minutes ❏ 1–3 hours ❏ 4–6 hours ❏ 7–9 hours

❏ 10–12 hours ❏ 13 hours or more

65. How many children in your home are more than 10 pounds overweight?

☐ 0   ☐ 1   ☐ 2   ☐ 3 or more

66. Do you have a child who has (or has had) an eating disorder? ☐ No ☐ Yes

67. What is a "kid favorite" breakfast at your home? (Be specific.)

Food: _____

68. List a child's favorite toy, activity, hobby, and game at your home:

Favorite toy: _____

Favorite activity: _____

Favorite hobby: _____

Favorite game: _____

69. Are your children involved in: (check all that apply)

☐ Music lessons   ☐ Sports

☐ Gifted programs   ☐ Poetry or recitation from memory

☐ Part-time employment   ☐ Agriculture clubs (4–H, FFA, FHA, etc.)

☐ Youth serving clubs (Scouts, Camp Fire Girls, etc.)

70. Would you or your children say they are "too busy"? ☐ No ☐ Yes

71. How much "downtime" (unplanned or free time) do your children experience per day?

☐ Less than 30 minutes   ☐ 30–60 minutes   ☐ 1–2 hours

☐ 2–4 hours   ☐ Over 4 hours

72. Do your children feel a need for "noise" in your home? If so, please write in how that noise is made! (If not, please leave blank.)

Activity: _____

Activity: _____

73. What would you say about your children's use of the computer compared to that of children who do watch TV?

☐ My children use the computer more

☐ It's about the same

☐ My children use it less because they are not used to passive entertainment

☐ I don't know

74. What is the most common substitute activity for TV among your children?

Activity: _____

75. How many days per week (on average) does your school-age child have organized activities before or after school?

☐ 0   ☐ 1   ☐ 2   ☐ 3   ☐ 4   ☐ 5   ☐ 6   ☐ 7

76. How many activities outside of school (on average) is your child involved in?

☐ 0   ☐ 1   ☐ 2   ☐ 3   ☐ 4   ☐ 5   ☐ 6   ☐ 7

77. How would you rank your school-age children for academic achievement? *(check all that apply)*

☐ All A's   ☐ Mostly A's   ☐ Mostly B's   ☐ Average   ☐ Below average

78. How many minutes per day (on average) would you say your child spends reading?

☐ Less than 15 minutes   ☐ 16–30 minutes   ☐ 31–60 minutes

☐ 60 minutes or more   ☐ Not reading yet

79. How many minutes per day (on average) do you spend reading to your children?

☐ Less than 15 minutes   ☐ 16–30 minutes   ☐ 31–60 minutes

☐ 60 minutes or more

80. How would you classify your child's reading capabilities? *(check all that apply)*

☐ Well above average   ☐ Above average   ☐ Average

☐ Below average   ☐ Well below average   ☐ Not reading yet

81. Do you feel the lack of TV in your home has been responsible for an improvement in your child's reading skills?

☐ Absolutely   ☐ Very likely   ☐ Not sure   ☐ Not likely   ☐ Not at all

82. Do your children seem to have more or fewer close friends than their classmates?

☐ More close friends   ☐ Same number   ☐ Fewer close friends

83. Do your children ever get teased by other children about not having or watching TV?

☐ Absolutely not   ☐ Not really   ☐ Could be   ☐ Somewhat   ☐ All the time

84. Do your children feel they are missing anything by not watching TV?

☐ Absolutely not   ☐ Not really   ☐ Could be   ☐ Somewhat   ☐ All the time

85. How often does your child pressure you to buy brand-name items and/or popular toys or games?

☐ All the time   ☐ Much of the time   ☐ Just like the rest of society

☐ Not too much   ☐ Rarely   ☐ Never

86. Name two of your children's heroes:

Hero: _____

Hero: _____

87. What are your children's top three activities on Sunday mornings?

Activity: _____

Activity: _____

Activity: _____

living outside the box

88. Do your children ever complain about the lack of TV in your home?

☐ All the time ☐ Sometimes ☐ Rarely

☐ Never ☐ Used to but not now

Part 5: The Community

89. Is your family involved in community service? ☐ No ☐ Yes

90. How many hours per month are devoted to community service?

☐ None ☐ 1–3 hours ☐ 4–7 hours

☐ 8–10 hours ☐ Over 10 hours

91. Do you know your neighbors very well? ☐ No ☐ Yes

92. How would you classify your family in regard to family rituals?

☐ We have few to none

☐ We celebrate birthdays and holidays only

☐ We have many others besides birthdays and holidays

☐ Rituals are a part of life—we have them nearly all the time!

93. What are your preferred methods of following world, national, and local news and sports? (Be specific: NPR, *Atlantic Monthly*, local newspaper, etc.)

Method: _____

Method: _____

94. On a scale of 1 to 10, with 1 being "not current" and 10 being "very current," how up to date are you with the national and local news?

☐ 1 ☐ 2 ☐ 3 ☐ 4 ☐ 5

☐ 6 ☐ 7 ☐ 8 ☐ 9 ☐ 10

95. Do you ever doubt your decision to not own a TV or to watch TV only rarely?

☐ Never ☐ Sometimes ☐ Quite often ☐ All the time

96. How would you rank your overall satisfaction with life?

☐ Very satisfied ☐ Somewhat satisfied

☐ Not very satisfied ☐ Not at all satisfied

Part 6: Your Stories, Values, and Dreams

Ahhh . . . you are almost finished! In the last three questions, feel free to mention your name if you would be willing to see your remarks appear in print at some later date. There is a space at the end of this survey for you to write in your name and phone number for future reference.

97. Please tell me "your story" about the big TV-free decision in your life. What has shaped your decision, and how do you feel about it? If you have recent memories of "turning it off," please add any tips you can offer on how to survive the first two weeks! Also include any advice you might give to others who are considering cutting back on TV viewing or getting rid of their TV.

Thoughts:

(Please attach an additional page if desired.)

The last two questions were suggested by well-known authors, **Mary Pipher** (author of *Reviving Ophelia* and *In the Shelter of Each Other*, both superb books on parenting and lifestyles today) and **Michael Gurian** (author of *A Fine Young Man* and *The Wonder of Boys*, two excellent, thought-provoking books on raising adolescent boys).

98. Mary Pipher would like to know about your children's values and dreams. In the space below, tell me what your children value most and what they want out of life.

Thoughts:

(Please attach an additional page if desired.)

99. Michael Gurian would like to know whether you feel you are "missing out." In the space below, tell me whether you feel you are missing anything in comparison to families who watch TV (and, if so, what)?

Thoughts:

(Please attach an additional page if desired.)

100. FINAL REQUEST: If you currently have or have raised adolescent children and would like to be involved in a study next year on TV-free adolescent behavior, please check your response to give me an idea of numbers! Thank you! ☐   No   ☐   Yes

Would you be available for a possible phone interview? If so, please include name and number:

Name: _____

Phone: _____

REMEMBER TO RETURN IN ENCLOSED ENVELOPE TO:
Dr. Barbara J. Brock
MS #66
Eastern Washington University
Cheney, WA 99004

Thank you so very much. Keep up the good work!

appendix b:
tv-free families
in america

In 2000, approximately five hundred families participated in the TV-free survey reproduced in Appendix A. The objective of my research was to paint a thick, descriptive picture of life without television. In addition to answers to the survey questions, I also received hundreds of pages of supplementary information, often in the form of extended essays. As an approach to organizing the wealth of data yielded by the survey, I formulated the following ten questions:

1. Who are these people?
2. What do they do with all that free time?
3. How do TV-free families keep up with news and sports?
4. Do TV-free individuals substitute computer and Internet use for TV watching?
5. Are TV-free children any different in terms of their academic performance, physical health, or social skills?
6. Do TV-free individuals feel they're missing out on anything by not watching television?
7. Who are their children's heroes?
8. How satisfied with life are these families?
9. Why did they decide to turn off the television?
10. How do they keep it off?

1. Who are these people?   *Summary*: The TV-free families who participated in the study spanned a wide range of income brackets and levels of education. Most were white, although various ethnic groups were represented. On average, TV-free couples were in their thirties or forties, with two children, held college degrees, and had a combined annual income of $40,000 to $60,000 and a savings plan. They owned a home in the suburbs and two cars. Two-thirds had some sort of religious affiliation. Fewer than half sent their kids to public schools.

17% of the adult respondents were between the ages of 20 and 30; 74% were between 31 and 50; and 9% were over 50.

80% of the respondents were female; 20% were male.

94% were married, and a total of 19% had been through a divorce.

32% had one child, 43% had two children, 16% had three, 4% had four, and 2% had more than four; the remaining 3% were childless.

Of the nearly five hundred children represented in the survey, 39% were 3 years old or younger, 39% were between the ages of 4 and 9, and 22% were 10 or older.

78% of the adults had college degrees. Their annual incomes ranged as follows:

$20,000 or less	4%	$80,000 to $99,999	17%
$20,000 to $39,999	20%	$100,000 to $129,999	7%
$40,000 to $59,000	20%	$130,000 or more	9%
$60,000 to $79,999	23%		

90% of the adults had a savings or retirement plan. Roughly a quarter of them were saving between 7% and 10% of their income each year, and another third were saving 11% or more. In addition, 75% of the children had savings accounts.

A majority of the respondents were white; the other ethnic groups represented were Latino, Asian American, Pacific Islander, Native American, and African American.

48% of the families consisted of a father who worked outside the home and a stay-at-home mother; another 25% consisted of one parent who worked full time and a second who worked part time; in another 15%, both parents were employed full time. The remainder comprised families in which the mother worked full time and the father stayed home; unmarried individuals, some of them employed full time, some part time, and some not employed; and retired couples or individuals.

86% of the respondents owned a house. Nearly half of the homeowners (49%) lived in the suburbs, 33% lived in rural areas, and 18% in urban settings.

65% of the families owned two cars. In addition, 45% of the respondents reported that they used some sort of commuter option for getting to work.

64% of the respondents owned a pet or pets; 88% were involved in gardening and/or recycling; 66% reported that they had a religious affiliation.

42% of the children attended public schools, 30% were enrolled in private schools, and 28% were schooled at home.

2. What do they do with all that free time?

Summary: Recreational activities covered a broad spectrum. Reading was at the top of the list for both children and adults, followed by engaging in conversation, for adults, and fantasy play, for kids. Other activities commonly mentioned were hobbies, games, home improvement, spending time with pets, going for walks and other outdoor activities, playing sports, listening to music, writing, gardening, going to the movies, having sit-down dinners and engaging in other family activities, making recreational use of the Internet, taking naps, having sex, and participating in community service. On average, couples reported spending almost an hour a day in meaningful conversation with their children and about three-quarters of an hour talking with their spouse or partner. Nearly 4 out of 5 adults felt that not having a TV had made their marriage stronger.

In reply to a question about how much free time the whole family spends together each day, 15% of the respondents said less than 30 minutes, 31% said 30 to 60 minutes, 37% said 1 to 2 hours, and 17% said over 2 hours.

According to their parents, 35% of children had over 4 hours of free time each day, another 35% had 2 to 4 hours, and the remaining 30% had less than 2 hours. When parents were asked whether they thought their children were "too busy," 90% responded "no," and 10% said "yes."

On average, parents reported spending 55 minutes in meaningful conversation with their children on a typical day.

Nearly a quarter of the families reported that they checked out over 20 books from the library every month; another 19% checked out 11 to 20 books a month.

Over 90% of the families said they sat down to dinner four or more times per week, with 43% of those dinners taking half an hour or longer.

35% of families went to the movies once or twice in a typical month, and 3% went three or four times; 62% claimed they never went to the movies.

Couples reported spending an average of 48 minutes in meaningful conversation with their spouse or partner each day, and 78% felt that their marriage was stronger because of the lack of television in their home.

73% of the families commented that birthday celebrations and holiday observances, along with other family rituals, were very common. Nearly half claimed that such rituals were a constant or near-constant part of family life.

31% of fathers and 25% of mothers reported that they were involved in a social group; 33% of fathers and 57% of mothers said they were members of two or more such groups.

81% of children were involved in sports, 73% in music, 58% in gifted programs, 56% in youth serving agencies, 47% in poetry or recitation from memory, 44% in part-time employment, and 43% in agricultural clubs (4-H, FFA, FHA, etc.).

Two-thirds of the families were active in community service, with half of those families putting in 1 to 3 hours a week and the other half volunteering 4 or more hours per week.

3: How do TV-free families keep up with news and sports?

Summary: Nearly three-quarters of the adult respondents felt they had no trouble keeping current with both national and local news, including sports. National Public Radio was by far the most popular source of news. In essay responses, respondents frequently voiced their strong preference for NPR radio news over TV news, with its tendency toward sensationalism and the endless repetition of certain stories.

When asked to indicate how up to date they were with local and national news, 70% of the respondents ranked themselves at least an 8 on a scale of 1 to 10 (with 10 being the highest).

National Public Radio was at the top of the list of news media, with local newspapers, other radio news, Internet news, and national newspapers and magazines following.

The most commonly mentioned national newspapers and magazines were the *New York Times*, the *Wall Street Journal*, *Time*, *Newsweek*, the *Atlantic Monthly*, *Discover*, and *Harper's Review*.

Sports fans listed the sports page of local newspapers and the sports news on radio as their chief sources of information. Several commented that they enjoyed being able to work on a project, whether indoors or outdoors, while they were listening to a favorite radio commentator covering a sports event.

4. Do TV-free individuals substitute computer and Internet use for TV watching?

Summary: Somewhat to my surprise, even though nearly all of the respondents owned at least one computer, most felt that the computer had not replaced the television as a source of entertainment. Of the adults, roughly two-thirds spent an average of no more than 3 hours a week making recreational use of the computer, and only 1 in 10 felt that they used the computer "too much." Moreover, only 7% of parents felt that their children spent too much time with the computer. Nearly 40% of the children in the survey were under the age of three, and so use of the computer was not yet an issue. About a third of those who were old enough to be using a computer played computer games, but typically for no more than 3 hours a week. In addition, some children used the Internet, and a few visited chat rooms with their friends. Nearly half of the parents said they felt their children made less use of the computer than did children who watch TV and pointed to the passive nature of the activity as an explanation. In essay responses, parents often mentioned that their children tended to find video games boring.

98% of families owned one or more computers.

15% of adults said they never used the computer for recreation, 50% said they spent 1 to 3 hours a week making recreational use of the computer, 28% spent between 4 and 9 hours, and 7% spent 10 or more hours a week.

Only 10% of adults felt they used the computer "too much"; 90% said they did not.

84% felt that the computer had not taken over the role of TV in their home, 8% said they weren't sure, and 8% felt it had.

Only 7% of parents felt that their children used the computer too much. About a third (32%) of TV-free children used the computer to play Nintendo or other games; the other 68% did not. Among the children who did play these games, 10% did so for less than 1 hour a week, 15% from 1 to 3 hours per week, 3% from 4 to 6 hours a week, 2% from 7 to 9 hours, and 2% for 10 hours or more.

According to their parents, 84% of children did not use the Internet. Of the 16% who did, 9% did so for less than an hour each week, 5% for 1 to 2 hours, 1.5% for 3 to 4 hours, and 0.5% for 7 to 9 hours. (None fell into the 5-to-6-hour range.)

Only 3% of children visited chat rooms with their friends: 2.2% "chatted" for 1 to 3 hours a week, 10.5 % for 4 to 6 hours, and 0.3% for 7 or more hours a week.

Only 7% of parents felt that their children used the computer too much; the other 93% did not.

When asked whether their children used the computer more or less often than children who watch TV, 45% of parents said they felt they used it less, owing to the passive nature of the activity; 7% said they felt it was about the same; 4% said they felt their children used it more. The remaining 44% said they did not know.

5. Are TV-free children any different in terms of their academic performance, physical health, or social skills?

Summary: TV-free children are readers. Approximately 4 out of 5 parents said that their children's reading skills were well above average or above average, and roughly 2 out of 5 of the children who were old enough to read did so for at least an hour a day. In addition, nearly half of TV-free parents spent at least 30 minutes a day reading to their children. A large majority felt that the lack of a TV in the home was responsible for their children's improved reading ability. Just over half of the children in TV-free households were A students.

TV-free children are active. Nearly a quarter of the children engaged in physical activity for 13 or more hours a week, and relatively few of them (7%) were more than 10 pounds overweight.

Some 7 out of 10 parents felt that their children got along better with each other without a TV in the house. Many parents remarked that their children were able to entertain themselves or play together for hours with fewer arguments. According to parents, TV-free children had about the same number of close friends as children who watch television and were rarely teased about not having a TV. A number of parents also commented that their children generally seemed at ease when interacting with adults outside the family.

Academic performance According to their parents, 51% of TV-free children received mostly A's or straight A's in school, 17% were earning B's, 17% were average students, and 15% were below average.

Reading capabilities were classified as well above or above average by 81% of the parents, as average by 15%, and as below average by 4%.

Of the children who were old enough to read, 41% read for at least an hour a day, 32% read from 31 to 60 minutes, 22% read from 16 to 30 minutes, and 5% read for 15 minutes or less.

45% of parents said they spent at least 30 minutes a day reading to their children, 36% said they spent between 16 and 30 minutes doing so, and 19% did so for 15 minutes or less.

83% of parents felt that the absence of TV from the household had fostered improved reading skills in their children, 11% said they weren't sure, and 6% said it had not or probably had not.

In more than two hundred of the essay responses, parents remarked that their children appeared to have much longer attention spans than did other children. Many parents also commented on the fact that, in the face of boredom, children's creativity and self-motivation often emerge.

Physical health   23% of the children spent 13 or more hours per week engaged in some sort of physical activity, 33% spent from 7 to 12 hours, 28% from 4 to 6 hours, 13% from 1 to 3 hours, and 3% less than an hour.

7% of the children represented were more than 10 pounds overweight.

Only 2% of the children had experienced an eating disorder.

Social skills   When parents who had more than one child were asked how much time their children spent interacting with one another, 33% said between 2 and 4 hours per day, 31% said between 1 and 2 hours, 22% between 30 and 59 minutes, 10% between 15 and 29 minutes, and 4% 14 minutes or less.

When asked whether they thought their children got along better with each other because there was no TV in the house, 70% of parents said "yes," 7% said "no," and 23% said they felt it made no difference. In their essay responses, parents often mentioned that their children were able to play together for long hours and seemed to have fewer sibling fights, given that there was no TV to fight over.

When asked whether they thought their children had more or fewer close friends than their classmates, 68% of parents said it seemed about the same, 22% felt their children had fewer close friends, and 10% felt they had more.

When asked whether their children were ever teased about not having a TV, 40% of parents answered "absolutely not," 37% answered "not really," and 23% answered "somewhat" or "could be."

In addition, a number of parents reported in essay responses that their children seemed surprisingly comfortable conversing and interacting with adults outside the immediate family.

Quite a few parents also remarked on the fact that their children had not particularly turned to outside activities to fill up the hours that they might otherwise have spent watching TV. Instead, these children simply had a good deal more unstructured free time at home than the average child, during which they tended to occupy themselves with ad hoc forms of play. Parents often mentioned that, in comparison to their peers, their children seemed to have longer attention spans and were able to entertain themselves for longer periods of time. One family mentioned their struggle with an ADD child. After they took their pediatrician's advice and removed the TV from their home, their child made tremendous developmental strides and, although still very active, was more able to channel energy in positive ways.

6. Do TV-free individuals feel they're missing out on anything by not watching television?

Summary: The overwhelming response was "no." Moreover, when parents were asked whether their children seemed to feel they were missing out by not watching TV, three-quarters responded "absolutely not" or "not really." Nearly 9 out of 10 said that their children "never" or "rarely" complained about not having a TV. Parents were also grateful to be "missing out" on TV commercials: only 1 in 20 indicated that their children pestered them to purchase brand-name products. A few respondents expressed some slight regret over the sacrifice of a favorite program, but they were quick to add that having time to spend on other things more than offset the loss. In fact, the vast majority of TV-free individuals felt that TV-watching families were the ones missing out . . . on life.

When asked whether their children felt they were missing out by not having a TV, 75% of parents replied "absolutely not" or "not really," 13% said "somewhat," 10% replied "could be," and 2% answered "all the time."

When asked whether their children ever complain about the lack of TV, 87% of parents answered "never" or "rarely," 6% said "used to but not now," and 7% answered "sometimes."

When parents were asked how often their children pressured them to buy brand-name items and/or popular toys or games, 78% answered "never" or "rarely," and 17% said "not too much." Of the remaining 5%, 4% said they thought it was about the same as elsewhere in our society, and 1% said their children did so "all the time."

A few adults commented that they occasionally regretted the loss of a favorite program or a good special on PBS or that they felt slightly out of it at times because they weren't up on the latest Ally McBeal gossip or hadn't seen the most recent episode of 911 or had missed a Discovery Channel program that other parents were talking about. But they also mentioned that if they listened in on a conversation or two or read a popular magazine or the entertainment news in the paper, this usually sufficed to keep them in touch with popular culture. In essay responses, TV-free individuals often indicated that they were glad *not* to have spent an hour of their previous evening getting to know some movie star or watching nature attempt to unfold on a two-dimensional screen. For them, real people and real experiences took precedence.

7. Who are their children's heroes? Hands down, Dad and Mom were the winners. Others receiving multiple votes were a child's teacher or coach, Harry Potter, Jesus, Martin Luther King Jr., Michael Jordan, grandma, grandpa, Winnie the Pooh, Robin Hood, Eleanor Roosevelt, Hermione (also from the Harry Potter books), and Laura Ingles (from the novel *Little House on the Prairie*).

8. How satisfied with life are these families? 81% of the respondents claimed that they were "very satisfied" with life, and close to another 19% said that they were "somewhat satisfied." Less than half of 1% said "not very satisfied."

9. Why did they decide to turn off the television? *Summary*: I received volumes of heartfelt replies from families who shared their reasons for making the choice to go TV free and the rewards they felt their decision had brought them. It is impossible to do them all justice. But the reasons they gave sounded three common themes: (1) to regain and retain a closeness of family, (2) to exert at least a small measure of control over what children are exposed to within the four walls of their home, and (3) to encourage dreams and stimulate creativity in themselves and in their children.

In order to qualify as TV free, respondents had to watch less than 6 hours of TV per week. A little over half (52%) watched absolutely no television. Of the remaining 48%, 19% watched less than 30 minutes a week, 8% watched from 30 to 60 minutes, 17% watched 1 to 2 hours, and 4% from 3 to 6 hours a week.

50% of the respondents had been TV free for over 7 years, and 40% for 1 to 6 years. The other 10% had given up TV within the past year.

When asked whether they ever questioned their decision not to own a television or to watch TV only rarely, 85% answered "never," and 15% answered "sometimes." In essay responses to this question, a number of specific reasons for the decision to go TV free received fairly frequent mention. Most commonly, respondents had simply decided to take back some time for themselves and their families in a busy world by getting rid of the television. Some were frustrated with the poor quality of standard TV fare or fed up with the violence and/or the incessant advertising. Others pointed to a lack of communication within the family or to the problems they had experienced trying to control their children's TV viewing.

Some came from homes that were literally saturated with TV and harbored sad memories of having felt ignored by their TV-watching parents; some resented the lack of family interaction. These respondents had chosen to live and raise their families in a completely different manner from that in which they were brought up.

In contrast, some had been raised without television or came from homes in which TV viewing had been severely restricted. Looking back, they decided they liked this lifestyle and opted to continue the tradition. Others never really made a conscious decision not to own a TV but, as young adults, had simply not gotten around to buying one. They gradually became aware that they liked life without television and realized, often when they themselves became parents, that they would prefer to keep it that way.

10. How do they keep it off?   Tips on how to go TV free included:

- Place the TV in a "hard to get to" place.
- Go cold turkey. ("Kids adapt within two weeks—
  if you can handle it!")
- Begin by stopping your subscription to cable service
  and then "graduate" to network.
- "Fix" the TV so that it only plays videos; then limit the
  number of videos.
- Have a yard sale and get rid of your TV and all your videos at
  the same time.
- Leave the TV behind every time you move.

Suggestions for coping included:

- Sit quietly with a cup of tea and think about what you really want to do before jumping into several new activities at once.
- Be patient. If you can live through twenty minutes of whining, your children *will* find something to do. Parents often commented that although getting rid of the TV led to increased child-care responsibilities for a week or two, what with children vying for attention, it actually lessened the burden of child care after their children got used to entertaining themselves.
- Send the kids outside. One man had a vivid memory of his mother standing at the kitchen door with her yellow-rubber-gloved hand pointing to the yard and booming, "Everyone outside until dinnertime!"
- Make a list of all the things you love to do besides watching TV and keep it posted somewhere.
- Come out of the closet—tell your friends what you are attempting. You may meet with more support than you think.
- At the same time, when friends and relatives ask what in the world are you doing, don't justify: just smile.
- Take photos of your children doing creative things and keep them visible.
- Go for a walk during your favorite sitcom, get your heart pumping, and breathe deeply.
- Create your *own* experiences rather than living vicariously. Instead of getting caught up in conversations that revolve around television, start working on building a life of your own. The best memories are born from what you do and what you share with others.
- Keep a journal of your withdrawal from television. It will make for good reading in only a few short weeks! You won't believe how much easier it gets with time.
- Finally, remember that people who have lived without television for any length of time often wonder out loud how the rest of the world finds time just to sit and watch.

appendix c: exercises and activities

1. Twenty Things I Love to Do   Begin by listing twenty things you love to do: write quickly, without a lot of thought. Then go back and complete the seven columns beside your list.

- In column 1, place a check beside the activities you did last week.
- In column 2, check any that cost over $5.00 each time you do them.
- In column 3, check those that require advance planning.
- In column 4, check those that you can do alone.
- In column 5, check any you will still do when you are 65 years old.
- In column 6, check any that are new within the past five years.
- In column 7, check activities that entail an element of risk.

Leisure activity	1	2	3	4	5	6	7
1.	☐	☐	☐	☐	☐	☐	☐
2.	☐	☐	☐	☐	☐	☐	☐
3.	☐	☐	☐	☐	☐	☐	☐
4.	☐	☐	☐	☐	☐	☐	☐
5.	☐	☐	☐	☐	☐	☐	☐
6.	☐	☐	☐	☐	☐	☐	☐
7.	☐	☐	☐	☐	☐	☐	☐
8.	☐	☐	☐	☐	☐	☐	☐
9.	☐	☐	☐	☐	☐	☐	☐
10.	☐	☐	☐	☐	☐	☐	☐
11.	☐	☐	☐	☐	☐	☐	☐
12.	☐	☐	☐	☐	☐	☐	☐
13.	☐	☐	☐	☐	☐	☐	☐

14._____ ☐ ☐ ☐ ☐ ☐ ☐ ☐
15._____ ☐ ☐ ☐ ☐ ☐ ☐ ☐
16._____ ☐ ☐ ☐ ☐ ☐ ☐ ☐
17._____ ☐ ☐ ☐ ☐ ☐ ☐ ☐
18._____ ☐ ☐ ☐ ☐ ☐ ☐ ☐
19._____ ☐ ☐ ☐ ☐ ☐ ☐ ☐
20._____ ☐ ☐ ☐ ☐ ☐ ☐ ☐

Are you satisfied with your choices? Enough risk? Too pricey? None are new? All require advance planning? How could you be more satisfied with your list?

Summarize below.

living outside the box

2. Family Fun Conduct interviews with the oldest members of your extended family—try to include at least one who is over 65 years old. Take a peek at both sides of your family, men and women. Prepare your questions, and allow plenty of time for those you interview to share their thoughts. You might want to send them the questions in advance, to give them time to ponder their replies before you conduct the interview.

Ask the following questions:

1. What were three of your favorite things to do as a child?

   a. _____

   b. _____

   c. _____

2. Do you remember a few of your favorite books?

3. What particular toys were your very favorites?

4. Can you describe to me your most memorable Christmas gift?

5. What are your three favorite activities today?

   a. _____

   b. _____

   c. _____

6. If you could give three tips to young people today, what would they be?

   a. _____

   b. _____

   c. _____

3. The One with the Most Toys Wins?

For the past twenty years, I have held discussions with my university students about the material possessions they own. In one exercise, students fill out a form on which they record their "Material Delights." After listing all their most cherished possessions, particularly recreation equipment, they are asked to answer several questions about those possessions. It's an eye-opening experience for all of us to see what things rule our lives, what their upkeep costs us, and, too often, how the enjoyment they provide is fairly minimal.

List your favorite possessions in the space below. Then, to the right of each possession, write in what the item cost when you purchased it, why you purchased it, when the last time you used it was, and how much it costs to maintain. Finally, indicate whether you feel the possession is worth having: rank the item on a scale of 1 ("not at all worth it") to 10 ("couldn't live without it").

Possession	What it cost	Why purchased	Last time used	Cost of maintaining	Worth it? (1–10)
1.					
2.					
3.					
4.					
5.					
6.					
7.					
8.					
9.					
10.					

4. My Space   In the space below, design a comfortable bedroom to meet all your needs.
You will eat and bathe elsewhere: just allow for sleeping and for educational and/or recreational items.

Do this exercise with other family members or good friends and compare the results. Makes a good discussion piece on what we value most.

5. My Parents Always . . . Hundreds of adults who took part in my study of TV-free households felt extremely satisfied with their decision to live without television and said they had never regretted their choice. If you are considering making such a choice, then rather than begin by worrying about how to fill up "empty" time, try instead to adjust your attitude. Start by believing that *anything* you do on your own—including doing "nothing"—has more intrinsic worth than whatever TV has to offer. Let your mind roam.

Gradually or suddenly, out of this "emptiness" will come a desire to *do* something—thoughts about what you would most enjoy. At that point, you can safely invest money, time, or other resources in that activity, as the desire for it came from within you. If you run out and buy a lot of supposedly entertaining items before you give up television, you will miss this period of reflection and probably just exhaust your pocketbook.

If you have a hard time believing that something like playing with the dog has more value than watching the six o'clock news, try this exercise:

Go ahead—to the best of your recollection, what were the top three activities your parents engaged in when you were a kid? And what will your children say about you?

1. My parents were always . . . (or fill out separately for your mom and dad):

    a._____

    b._____

    c. _____

2. My children will say, "My parents were always . . ."

    a._____

    b._____

    c. _____

Wouldn't almost any answer sound better than "watching TV"?

6. My Kids Tend to . . . How do you see your children and their future? Are your kids developing good social and leisure skills? Can they fill an hour of free time with something that they (and you) would be proud of? Do they often rely on you to suggest activities? The children involved in my TV-free survey seemed much less prone to boredom than most children and were generally able to occupy themselves for hours with any number of recreational activities: building something, fantasy play, outdoor pursuits, artwork, music, reading, games of one sort or another, and so on. Take a break from screens, as the children who participated in "30 Days Live" did, and you may be surprised at the number of interests that suddenly blossom when at last you have time for reflection, decision, and action. Boredom is so often a springboard to creativity!

Go ahead—think about your children's favorite activities, the free time they have before and after school and how they spend it, and their customary weekend activities. Fill in your answers below.

If my children had one free hour in which to do whatever they wanted to do, they would:

Typical before-school activities for my kids are:

After school, my kids:

On Saturday mornings, my kids tend to:

Three of the main recreational activities my kids are involved in over the weekends are:

1._____
2._____
3. _____

Are you satisfied, and do you think your children are?
If not, it is never too late to change a habit!

living outside the box

7. Before I Die

Write in the year of your birth and the hypothetical year of your death, and then place an "X" on the line to represent where you are at this moment in your life.

19___ _____ 20___

List three major, very specific things you wish to do or accomplish before you die and then decide *the actual year* you will do them.

1. _____ Date: _____
   _____

2. _____ Date: _____
   _____

3. _____ Date: _____
   _____

Place the number and date of your goal on the timeline.

Now . . . what do you need to do today in order to get started? Write some advice to yourself in the space provided:

8. A Waking Experience

Before you start, place a sheet of paper over this page so that the questions can be revealed one by one. Write the answer to each question on that sheet of paper. When you've finished, staple your answer sheet to the questions and keep for future reference. It can be fun to do this exercise with a friend!

1. It is _____ (write the current month and day here), and the year is _____ (add twenty years to the current year). Your alarm goes off. How old are you? _____ You stretch, open your eyes, climb out of bed, and walk to the window of your bedroom. What do you see out the window? What do you put on to wear? What do you have for breakfast? And who, if anyone, is across the table from you?

2. You begin your day. Do you work outside the home? Travel to work? If so, how?

3. If you work outside the home, does anyone greet you when you arrive? What are some special things in your home or office? What are the first projects you work on?

4. Lunchtime! What do you do? With whom? How long a break do you have?

5. Afternoon begins. How do you feel? What are the tasks you take on in the afternoon? What are your "favorite" tasks of the day?

6. If you've been away from the house, what do you do on the way home, and what time do you arrive? What is the first thing you do upon entering your house? The second thing? When do you eat dinner, and what do you have? Describe your late afternoon and evening recreation activities. What time do you go to bed?

7. Are you finding time to enjoy your own leisure? Name two favorite activities at this point in your life.

a. _____

b. _____

8. Give three pieces of advice to your younger self, twenty years earlier.

a. _____

b. _____

c. _____

9. Finally, if you had to write an epitaph for your gravestone after a very long and productive life, what would you want it to say?

notes

Introduction: Out of the Closet

1. Nielsen Media Research, press release, August 21, 2006. Cited in "TVs Outnumber People in Most U.S. Homes," *Spokesman-Review* (Spokane), September 22, 2006. Statistics for 2000 are also from Nielsen Media Research and have been widely reported.

2. Victoria J. Rideout, Elizabeth A. Vandewater, and Ellen A. Wartella, *Zero to Six: Electronic Media in the Lives of Infants, Toddlers, and Preschoolers*, p. 4.

3. Valery Fahey, "TV by the Numbers," *Health*, December–January 1992, p. 35; U.S. Department of Education, "Strong Families, Strong Schools: Building Community Partnerships for Learning" (1994). These statistics appear in "Facts and Figures About Our TV Habit," an online resource maintained by the Center for Screen-Time Awareness (formerly the TV-Turnoff Network): see sec. I, no. 8, and sec. II, no. 15. The list is updated periodically, and each item is keyed to a source in the "Source Key" at the end of the document. The full URL for the page appears in the bibliography under "Center for Screen-Time Awareness," but the page—which is definitely worth a look—can also be accessed by going to http://www.tvturnoff.org/factsheets and selecting "Facts and Figures About Our TV Habit."

4. Barbara Cornell, "Pulling the Plug on TV," *Time*, October 16, 2000, p. F16.

Chapter 1: The Rise (and Fall) of Recreation

1. Gary Cross, *Social History of Leisure Since 1600*, p. 182.

2. R. F. Knapp, "Play for America: The New Deal and the NRA," cited in Ruth V. Russell, *Pastimes: The Context of Contemporary Leisure*, p. 268.

3. Cross, *Social History of Leisure Since 1600*, p. 181.

4. Ibid., pp. 183–84.

5. Ibid., p. 184.

6. See Nash, *Philosophy of Recreation and Leisure*, p. 89, for a drawing of the model, as well as the discussion on pp. 93–95.

7. Ibid., p. 93.

8. Jim Trelease, *The Read-Aloud Handbook*, p. 197.

Chapter 2: Fear of Leisure

1. John P. Robinson and Geoffrey Godbey, *Time for Life: The Surprising Ways Americans Use Their Time*, p. 231.

2. Marie Winn, *The Plug-In Drug*, p. 285.

3. According to a report from the Kaiser Family Foundation, *Kids and Media at the New Millennium*, as of 1999 the average American child lived in a home equipped with three TVs, three tape players, three radios, two CD players, two VCRs, a video game player, and a computer. See http://www.kff.org/entmedia/1535-index.cfm, under "Fact Sheet." For the relative prevalence of various media in the homes of children under the age of six as of 2006, see Victoria Rideout and Elizabeth Hamel, *The Media Family: Electronic Media in the Lives of Infants, Toddlers, Preschoolers, and Their Parents*, pp. 17–18.

4. Seth Borenstein, "Kids' Level of Inactivity Surprises Even Experts," *Spokesman-Review* (Spokane), August 22, 2003.

5. Victoria J. Rideout, Elizabeth A. Vandewater, and Ellen A. Wartella, *Zero to Six: Electronic Media in the Lives of Infants, Toddlers, and Preschoolers*, p. 4.

6. See Donald F. Roberts, Ulla G. Foehr, and Victoria Rideout, *Generation M: Media in the Lives of 8- to 18-Year-olds*, Table 5-B, p. 37. The authors provide a breakdown by specific types of media in Appendix 5.1, p. 132.

7. Robert Putnam, *Bowling Alone: The Collapse and Revival of American Community*, p. 224. Putnam's book-length study is based on his groundbreaking article "Bowling Alone: America's Declining Social Capital" (*Journal of Democracy* 6, no. 1 [January 1995]: 65–78).

8. *All Things Considered,* National Public Radio, May 31, 2000 (transcript of interview).

9. Hemingway cited in Ruth V. Russell, *Pastimes: The Context of Contemporary Leisure*, p. 18.

10. Jay B. Nash, *Philosophy of Recreation and Leisure*, p. 21.

11. See Mihaly Csikszentmihalyi, *Finding Flow*, pp. 64–65.

12. Ellen Neuborne, "Firms Today Less Willing to Pay for Play," *USA Today*, March 21, 1997.

13. Joe Robinson, "The Incredible Shrinking Vacation," in de Graaf, ed., *Take Back Your Time*, pp. 21, 22.

14. Juliet Schor, *The Overworked American*, p. 161.

15. John de Graaf, personal communication, January 15, 2006.

16. Putnam's remarks can be found at http://www.bettertogether.org/aboutthereport.htm. See also Ro-bert D. Putnam and Lewis M. Feldstein, *Better Together: Restoring the American Community* (New York: Simon & Schuster, 2003).

Chapter 3: A Word from Our Sponsors

1. John de Graaf, David Wann, and Thomas Naylor, *Affluenza: The All-Consuming Epidemic*, p. 154.

2. See "AAAA/ANA Annual Study Shows TV Clutter Levels Up Across Most Dayparts," press release from the Association of National Advertisers, February 14, 2002 (http//:www.ana.net/news/2002/02_14_02.cfm), reporting on the findings of the *2001 Television Commercial Monitoring Report* (New York: American Association of Advertising Agencies, 2002). Ironically, the advertising industry is concerned about commercial "clutter" because it tends to diminish the effectiveness of each individual ad.

3. Eugene Halton quoted in John Monczunski, "Spent," *Notre Dame Magazine Online*, Summer 2003.

4. Ibid.

5. Zachary A. Smith, *The Environmental Policy Paradox*, 4th ed. (New York: Prentice-Hall, 2003), p. 182.

6. de Graaf, Wann, and Naylor, *Affluenza*, p. 21. Statistics are reported in the documentary *Affluenza* (1997), produced by John de Graaf and Vivia Boe for KCTS/Seattle and Oregon Public Broadcasting and available on DVD from Bullfrog Films.

7. See de Graaf, Wann, and Naylor, *Affluenza*, pp. 21–22. The authors cite Steve Lohr, "Maybe It's Not All Your Fault," *New York Times*, December 5, 2004.

8. Ibid., pp. 19–20. The figures for credit card debt can be found in the U.S. Census Bureau's *Statistical Abstract*, 2004–5.

9. Ibid., p. 20. The statistics are from *Now with Bill Moyers*, February 6, 2004. Moyers was interviewing Elizabeth Warren, coauthor (with Amelia Warren Tyagi) of *The Two-Income Trap: Why Middle-Class Mothers and Fathers Are Going Broke*. A transcript of the interview is available at http://www.pbs.org/now/transcript/transcript306_full.html.

10. Mary Pipher, "All That Glitters," available at http://www.newdream.org/column/5.html.

11. Center for a New American Dream, "Thanks to Ads, Kids Won't Take No, No, No, No, No, No, No, No for an Answer," available at http://www.newdream.org/kids/poll.php.

12. Center for a New American Dream, "Tips for Parenting in a Commercial Culture," p. 6.

13. Center for a New American Dream, "Thanks to Ads, Kids Won't Take No, No, No, No, No, No, No, No for an Answer"; Miriam H. Zoll, "Psychologists Challenge Ethics of Marketing to Children," American News Service, April 5, 2000, available at http://www.mediachannel.org/originals/kidsell.shtml. See also Victor Greto, "Ad Nauseam," *The Gazette* (Colorado Springs), August 19, 1997, "Life" section, p. 1.

14. Zarghami quoted in Kim Masters, "For Toddlers, a World Laden with Advertising," available at http://www.npr.org/templates/story/ story.php?storyId=5569423.

15. See Dale Kunkel, "Children and Television Advertising," in *Handbook of Children and the Media*, ed. Dorothy G. Singer and Jerome L. Singer, pp. 375–93. See also "Television Advertising Leads to Unhealthy Habits in Children, Says APA Task Force," APA Online, February 23, 2004, available at http://www.apa.org/releases/childrenads.html.

16. "The Merchants of Cool" aired on February 27, 2001. Rushkoff's comments are from an interview concerning the show, available at http://www.pbs.org/wgbh/pages/frontline/shows/cool/interviews/rushkoff.html.

17. Roy F. Fox, *Harvesting Minds: How TV Commercials Control Kids*, p. 19.

18. Kanner quoted in Rebecca A. Clay, "Advertising to Children: Is It Ethical?" *Monitor on Psychology* 31, no. 8 (September 2000), available at http://www.apa.org/monitor/sep00/advertising.html.

19. Schor cited in Center for a New American Dream, "Tips for Parenting in a Commercial Culture," p. 14. See also Juliet Schor, *Born to Buy: The Commercialized Child and the New Consumer Culture*, pp. 167–72.

20. Center for Commercial-Free Public Education, "Channel One," available at http://www.ibiblio.org/commercialfree/channelonetext.html. The research in question was carried out by Alex Molnar, of the Center for the Analysis of Commercialism in Education at the University of Wisconsin–Milwaukee, and Max Sawicky, of the Economic Policy Institute.

21. James Steyer, *The Other Parent: The Inside Story of the Media's Effect on Our Children*, pp. 169–70 (the quotation is from p. 169).

22. Ibid., p. 269.

23. Dale Kunkel quoted in "Television Advertising Leads to Unhealthy Habits in Children, Says APA Task Force," APA Online, February 23, 2004, available at http://www.apa.org/releases/childrenads.html.

24. American Academy of Pediatrics, Committee on Public Education, "Children, Adolescents, and Television," *Pediatrics* 107, no. 2 (February 2001): 423.

25. Schor, *Born to Buy*, p. 13.

Chapter 4: How to Miss Nothing

1. "Bob and Mike Ryan: Identical Twin Doubles Champs," *Sports Illustrated*, August 28, 2006, p. 32.

2. For Rushkoff's comments, and the complete interview, see http://www.pbs.org/wgbh/pages/frontline/shows/cool/interviews/rushkoff.html.

3. John Monczunski, summarizing the views of sociologist Eugene Halton, "Spent," *Notre Dame Magazine Online*, Summer 2003.

Chapter 5: The Decision to Go TV Free

1. I should perhaps point out that the question about the rate of lovemaking was optional. All the same, over 50 percent of the couples who responded to the survey replied to it. It certainly piqued my husband's curiosity. He kept asking, "So how's it going with question 28?"

Chapter 6: Regarding Our Children

1. See "A Not-So Minor Risk," *Washington Post*, December 2, 2003, pp. F1, 3, and Henry J. Kaiser Family Foundation, "The Role of Media in Childhood Obesity," publication no. 7030, February 2004, available at http://www.kff.org/entmedia/upload/The-Role-of-Media-in-Childhood-Obesity.pdf.

2. Seth Borenstein, quoting CDC health scientist Marian Huhman, "Kids' Level of Inactivity Surprises Even Experts," *Spokesman-Review* (Spokane), August 22, 2003.

3. David Ruskin quoted in Sharon Kennedy Wynne, "TV Fit for Kids," *St. Petersburg Times* (Tampa Bay), January 24, 2006, available at http://www.sptimes.com/2006/01/24/news_pf/Floridian/TV_fit_for_kids.shtml. Similarly, according to the American Academy of Pediatrics, the increasing prevalence of obesity and inactivity among children poses an "unprecedented burden in terms of children's health as well as present and future health care costs." See American Academy of Pediatrics, Committee on Nutrition, "Policy Statement: Prevention of Pediatric Overweight and Obesity," *Pediatrics* 112 (August 2003): 424–30 (the quotation is from p. 424).

4. See William Dietz and Stephen Gortmaker, "Do We Fatten Our Children at the TV Set? Obesity and Television Viewing in Children and Adolescents," *Pediatrics* 75 (May 1985): 807–12.

5. See Dale Kunkel, "Children and Television Advertising," in *Handbook of Children and the Media*, ed. Dorothy G. Singer and Jerome L. Singer, pp. 375–93.

6. Center for Screen-Time Awareness, "Turn Off TV, Turn On a Healthier Lifestyle," available at http://www.tvturnoff.org/images/facts&figs/factsheets/HealthyLife.pdf.

7. See Dina L. G. Borzekowski and Thomas N. Robinson, "The 30-Second Effect: An Experiment Revealing the Impact of Television Commercials on Food Preferences of Preschoolers," *Journal of the American Dietary Association* 101, no. 1 (January 2001): 42–46.

8. Dr. David Satcher's comment is quoted in Center for Screen-Time Awareness, "Turn Off TV, Turn On a Healthier Lifestyle." For the statistics, see the Henry J. Kaiser Family Foundation, "The Role of Media in Childhood Obesity." As the KFF report explains, according to the CDC, children

are overweight if their weight is above the 95th percentile for their sex and age. Those whose weight falls between the 85th and 95th percentiles are deemed "at risk of being overweight."

9. See Lauran Neergaard, "Fight Against Childhood Obesity Found Wanting," *Spokesman-Review* (Spokane), September 14, 2006, p. A8.

10. Daniel B. Wood, "California Says 'No' to Junk-Food Sales in Schools," *Christian Science Monitor*, September 6, 2005, available at http://www.csmonitor.com/2005/0906/p02s01-uspo.htm. See also State of California, Department of Health Services, *California Obesity Prevention Plan: A Vision for Tomorrow, Strategic Actions for Today* (2006), available at http://www.dhs.ca.gov/CAObesityPrevention/.

11. "TV Fit for Kids," *St. Petersburg Times* (Tampa Bay), January 24, 2006, available at http://www.sptimes.com/2006/01/24/news_pf/Floridian/TV_fit_for_kids.shtml.

12. "Write to Save Your Kids," *Chicago Parent*, October 2005, available at http://www.chicagoparent.com/print.asp?ArticleID=5928& SectionID=20&SubSectionID=88.

13. Diane Levin quoted in "Cartoon Network's 'Tickle U' Is No Laughing Matter: CCFC Urges Families to Stay Away from New Preschool Programming," available at http://www.commercialexploitation.org/pressreleases/tickleu.htm.

14. American Academy of Pediatrics, Committee on Public Education, "Media Education," *Pediatrics* 104, no. 2 (August 1999): 342.

15. Robert Kubey and Mihaly Csikszentmihalyi, "Television Addiction Is No Mere Metaphor," p. 78, summarizing the work of Annie Lang and her colleagues at Indiana University. For Lang's research, see Annie Lang, "The Limited Capacity Model of Mediated Message Processing, *Journal of Communication* 50, no. 1 (March 2000): 46–70.

16. Jane M. Healey, *Endangered Minds: Why Children Don't Think—and What We Can Do About It*, p. 228.

17. Dimitri A. Christakis, Frederick J. Zimmerman, David L. DiGiuseppe, and Carolyn A. McCarty, "Early Television Exposure and Subsequent Attentional Problems in Children," *Pediatrics* 113, no. 4 (April 2004): 710.

18. See Claudia Wallis, "Blame It on *Teletubbies*," *Time*, October 30, 2006. It was the suggested link between TV and ADD that put economist Michael Waldman in mind of the alarming rise in the rates of autism over the past several decades (from 1 in 2,500 in 1970 to 1 in 170 today). Could TV be the culprit? In seeking to test this hypothesis, however, Waldman and his colleagues faced a problem, namely, the dearth of reliable information, on a sufficiently large scale, about the TV-viewing habits of children aged 1 to 3. Instead, they resorted to two indirect measures: the number of cable subscriptions in a given area—the assumption being that as more and more homes got cable, more and more small children were likely to be watching television—and

living outside the box

greater levels of rainfall, which other studies had already correlated with an increase in TV viewing. On this basis, they claimed to have discovered a link between heavy television viewing among toddlers and the incidence of autism—a claim that clearly rests on less than firm methodological foundations. "Could there be something to this strange piece of statistical derring-do?" Wallis wonders. "It's not impossible, but it would take a lot more research to tease out its true significance" (p. 65).

19. Zimmerman quoted in "Seattle Study of Kids Links Bullying to TV," *Seattle Times*, April 5, 2005. For the study itself, see Frederick J. Zimmerman, Gwen M. Glew, Dimitri A. Christakis, and Wayne Katon, "Early Cognitive Stimulation, Emotional Support, and Television Watching as Predictors of Subsequent Bullying Among Grade-School Children," *Archives of Pediatrics and Adolescent Medicine* 159, no. 4 (April 2005): 384–88.

20. American Academy of Pediatrics, Committee on Public Education, "Media Education," *Pediatrics* 104, no. 2 (August 1999): 341.

21. Brad J. Bushman and L. Rowell Huesmann, "Short-term and Long-term Effects of Violent Media on Aggression in Children and Adults," *Archives of Pediatrics and Adolescent Medicine* 160, no. 4 (April 2006): 351.

22. On the SMART program, see John Flesher, "Turning Off TV Makes U.P. Kids Less Aggressive," *Lansing State Journal*, January 28, 2006.

23. See Thomas N. Robinson et al., "Effects of Reducing Children's Television and Video Game Use on Aggressive Behavior: A Randomized Controlled Trial."

24. See Barbara A. Dennison, Theresa J. Russo, Patrick A. Burdick, and Paul L. Jenkins, "An Intervention to Reduce Television Viewing by Preschool Children," *Archives of Pediatrics and Adolescent Medicine* 158, no. 2 (February 2004): 170–76.

25. Marie Winn, *The Plug-In Drug*, pp. 4–5.

26. Donald Shifrin, "Effect of Media on Children and Adolescents: It's About Time," *Archives of Pediatrics and Adolescent Medicine* 106, no. 4 (April 2006): 449.

27. Winn, *Plug-In Drug*, p. 5.

28. Victoria J. Rideout, Elizabeth A. Vandewater, and Ellen A. Wartella, *Zero to Six: Electronic Media in the Lives of Infants, Toddlers, and Preschoolers*, p. 4.

29. Victoria J. Rideout and Elizabeth Hamel, *The Media Family: Electronic Media in the Lives of Infants, Toddlers, Preschoolers, and Their Parents*, p. 14.

30. Ibid., p. 5.

31. Rideout, Vandewater, and Wartella, *Zero to Six*, p. 4.

32. Rideout and Hamel, *The Media Family*, pp. 5, 18.

33. Healy quoted in Carrie McLaren, "Endangered Minds: An Interview with Jane Healy," *Stay Free!* no. 18 (Spring 2001), available at http://www.stayfreemagazine.org/archives/18/healy.html.

34. Donald F. Roberts, Ulla G. Foehr, and Victoria Rideout, *Generation M: Media in the Lives of 8- to 18-Year-olds*, pp. 19, 112, and 44.

35. See "TV Viewing and Children's Health," in the California Obesity Prevention Initiative (State of California, Department of Health Services), "Do More, Watch Less," p. 29. The COPI publication is available for download at http://www.dhs.ca.gov/ps/cdic/copi/copiforms/tvtool. htm. Concerning media time and academic performance, see, for example, Ariel R. Chernin and Deborah L. Linebarger, "The Relationship Between Children's Television Viewing and Academic Performance," *Archives of Pediatrics and Adolescent Medicine* 159, no. 7 (July 2005): 687–89; and "New Study Shows Excessive Media Screen Time Affects Kids' Grades," *USA Religious News*, October 5, 2006, available at http://www.usareligiousnews.com/newsArticle.php?ID=1125.

36. In 2000, a Nielsen survey found that, on average, children watched about 1,023 hours of television a year—a statistic that has been widely cited. The children surveyed in the *Generation M* study spent an average of 3 hours and 4 minutes a day watching television, which is the equivalent of 1,119 hours a year. When the average time devoted to videos or DVDs (47 minutes) and movies (25 minutes) was factored in, the amount of screen time rose to a total of 4 hours and 15 minutes daily—about 1,350 hours a year. See Roberts, Foehr, and Rideout, *Generation M: Media in the Lives of 8- to 18-Year-olds*, p. 23 and Table 4-A (p. 24). It is generally estimated that children spend about 900 hours a year in school.

37. Roberts, Foehr, and Rideout, *Generation M: Media in the Lives of 8- to 18-Year-olds*, pp. 25 and 37–38. Note that the questions about homework and chores were asked only of children in grades 7 to 12.

38. Ibid., p. 19.

39. Ibid., pp. 13 and 41.

40. Ibid., p. 132.

41. Ibid., pp. 53–54, and see also pp. 35–37 and p. 139.

42. Drew Altman quoted in a Kaiser Family Foundation press release, available at http://www.kff.org/entmedia/entmedia030905nr.cfm. The press release offers a useful summary of the *Generation M* findings. For an excellent overview of the research, see also "Children, TV, Computers and More Media: New Research Shows Pluses, Minuses," a press release issued on February 11, 2005, by the National Science Foundation, available at http://www.nsf.gov/news/news_summ.jsp?cntn_id=102813&org=nsf&from=news.

43. Claudia Wallis, "The Multitasking Generation," *Time*, March 27, 2006, p. 53.

44. Ibid., pp. 52–53.

45. "Report: Kids Don't Need Too Much Technology Ed," *Spokesman-Review* (Spokane), October 1, 2004, p. A8.

46. Carrie McLaren, "Endangered Minds: An Interview with Jane Healy," *Stay Free!* no. 18 (Spring 2001), available at http://www.stayfreemagazine.org/archives/18/healy.html.

47. Hallowell quoted in Claudia Wallis, "The Multitasking Generation," p. 55.

48. American Academy of Pediatrics, Committee on Public Education, "Children, Adolescents, and Television," *Pediatrics* 107, no. 2 (February 2001): 424.

49. Rideout and Hamel, *The Media Family*, p. 16.

50. American Family Research Council, "Parents Fight 'Time Famine' as Economic Pressures Increase" (1990). Cited in Center for Screen-Time Awareness, "Facts and Figures About Our TV Habit," sec. I, no. 9.

51. *Scholastic News*, April 22, 2004. The results of the survey were posted at http://teacher.scholastic.com/scholasticnews/vote/results.asp, but are no longer available on the site.

52. Billy Tashman, "Sorry Ernie, TV Isn't Teaching," *New York Times*, November 12, 1994. Cited in Center for Screen-Time Awareness, "Facts and Figures About Our TV Habit," sec. II, no. 16.

Chapter 7: Thirty Days Without Television

1. In 2003, 56 students participated in "30 Days Live," 43 of whom (77%) made it through the entire month. In 2005, 74 students participated, and 58 (78%) lasted the duration.

2. Out of the total of 130 students who took part in the two studies, 69 (53%) predicted success, and 56 of them (81%) were proved correct. The other 61 students (47%) predicted failure, but 44 of them (72%) actually succeeded. The statistical breakdown was as follows. Of the 56 students who were involved in the 2003 study, 31 (55%) predicted success, and 25 of them (80%) did indeed make it through the month. The other 25 (45%) predicted failure, but 17 of them (68%) also made it. In 2005, 38 of the 74 students (51%) predicted success, and 30 (79%) were proved correct. The remaining 36 (49%) predicted failure, but 27 of them (75%) also ended up succeeding.

3. By the halfway point, a total of 21 students had quit: 9 out of the 56 participants in 2003 and 12 out of the 74 in 2005. By the end, another 9 had dropped out: 5 in 2003 and 4 in 2005. In all, then, out of the 130 participants overall, 30 (23%) failed to last the entire thirty days—and 21 of these 30 (70%) quit before the halfway point. The attrition rate was thus higher during the first two weeks than the second.

4. Jack Mingo, "TV in America," *The Official Couch Potato Handbook*, reprinted in the *Wilson Quarterly*, Autumn 1992, p. 44. Cited in Center for Screen-Time Awareness, "Facts and Figures About Our TV Habit," sec. I, no. 10.

Chapter 8: Breaking the Soft Addiction

1. Robert Kubey and Mihaly Csikszentmihalyi, "Television Addiction Is No Mere Metaphor," *Scientific American*, February 2002, p. 76.

2. Ibid.

3. Valery Fahey, "TV by the Numbers, *Health*, December–January 1992, p. 35.

4. Kubey and Csikszentmihalyi, "Television Addiction Is No Mere Metaphor," p. 77.

5. Ibid., p. 76.

6. Ibid., p. 79.

7. Ibid. The study to which Kubey and Csikszentmihalyi refer is T. M. Williams and A. G. Hanford, "Television and Other Leisure Activities," in *The Impact of Television: A Natural Experiment in Three Communities*, ed. T. M. Williams, pp. 143–213 (Orlando: Academic Press, 1986). For a useful summary of the research, see the review by John Redford available at http://www.theworld.com/~jlr/comment/tv_impact.htm.

8. Barbara J. Brock, J. Hammermeister, D. Winterstein, and R. Page, "Life Without TV? Cultivation Theory and Psychosocial Characteristics of Television-Free Individuals and Their Television-Viewing Counterparts," *Health Communication* 17, no. 3 (2005): 253–64.

9. Kubey and Csikszentmihalyi, "Television Addiction Is No Mere Metaphor," p. 79. Steiner's work can be found in Gary A. Steiner, *The People Look at Television: A Study of Audience Attitudes* (New York: Knopf, 1963).

10. Ibid., p. 80.

Chapter 10: Time for Reflection

1. See Sherry Stripling, "Is It Any Wonder Americans Want Their Time Back?" *Seattle Times*, October 12, 2003. The figures are from the International Labor Organization, the United Nations' labor agency.

2. Richard Seven, "Life Interrupted: Plugged into It All, We're Stressed to Distraction," *Pacific Northwest: The Seattle Times Magazine*, November 28, 2004, available at http://seattletimes.nwsource.com/pacificnw/2004/1128/cover.html.

3. McKibben and Levy quoted in Jeffrey Young, "Knowing When to Log Off: Wired Campuses May Be Causing 'Information Overload,'" *Chronicle of Higher Education*, April 22, 2005, available at http://chronicle.com/free/v51/i33/33a03401.htm.

4. Robert Putnam, *Bowling Alone: The Collapse and Revival of American Community*, p. 231.

bibliography

American Academy of Pediatrics. "Television and the Family: Guidelines for Parents." Pamphlet. Elk Grove Village, IL: AAP Division of Publications, 1995.

———. Committee on Public Education. "Media Education." *Pediatrics* 104, no. 2 (August 1999): 341–43.

———. Committee on Public Education. "Children, Adolescents, and Television." *Pediatrics* 107, no. 2 (February 2001): 423–46.

Borenstein, Seth. "Kids' Level of Inactivity Surprises Even Experts." *Spokesman-Review* (Spokane), August 22, 2003.

Borzekowski, Dina L. G., and Thomas N. Robinson. "The 30-Second Effect: An Experiment Revealing the Impact of Television Commercials on Food Preferences of Preschoolers." *Journal of the American Dietary Association* 101, no. 1 (January 2001): 42–46.

Brock, Barbara J. "Life Without Television." *Parks and Recreation*, November 2002, pp. 68–72.

Brock, Barbara J., J. Hammermeister, D. Winterstein, and R. Page. "Life Without TV? Cultivation Theory and Psychosocial Characteristics of Television-Free Individuals and Their Television-Viewing Counterparts." *Health Communication* 17, no. 3 (2005): 253–64.

Bushman, Brad J., and L. Rowell Huesmann. "Short-term and Long-term Effects of Violent Media on Aggression in Children and Adults." *Archives of Pediatrics and Adolescent Medicine* 160, no. 4 (April 2006): 348–52.

Center for a New American Dream. "Tips for Parenting in a Commercial Culture." Pamphlet. April 2006.

Center for Screen-Time Awareness. "Facts and Figures About Our TV Habit." Available at http://www.tvturnoff.org/images/facts&figs/factsheets/FactsFigs.pdf

———. "Turn Off TV, Turn On a Healthier Lifestyle." Available at http://www.tvturnoff.org/images/facts&figs/factsheets/HealthyLife.pdf

Chamberlain, Lisa J., Yun Wang, and Thomas N. Robinson. "Does Children's Screen Time Predict Requests for Advertised Products? Cross-sectional and Prospective Analyses." *Archives of Pediatrics and Adolescent Medicine* 160, no. 4 (April 2006): 363–68.

Chernin, Ariel R., and Deborah L. Linebarger. "The Relationship Between Children's Television Viewing and Academic Performance." *Archives of Pediatrics and Adolescent Medicine* 159, no. 7 (July 2005): 687–89.

Christakis, Dimitri A., Frederick J. Zimmerman, David L. DiGiuseppe, and Carolyn A. McCarty. "Early Television Exposure and Subsequent Attentional Problems in Children." *Pediatrics* 113, no. 4 (April 2004): 708–13.

Clay, Rebecca A. "Advertising to Children: Is It Ethical?" *Monitor on Psychology* 31, no. 8 (September 2000). Available at http://www.apa.org/monitor/sep00/advertising.html

Cornell, Barbara. "Pulling the Plug on TV." *Time*, October 16, 2000, p. F16. Available at http://www.time.com/time/archive/preview/0,10987,1101001016-91805,00.html

Cross, Gary. *Social History of Leisure Since 1600.* State College, PA: Venture Publishing, 1990.

Csikszentmihalyi, Mihaly. *Finding Flow: The Psychology of Engagement with Everyday Life.* New York: HarperCollins, 1997.

de Graaf, John, ed. *Take Back Your Time: Fighting Overwork and Time Poverty in America.* San Francisco: Berrett-Koehler Publishers, 2003.

de Graaf, John, David Wann, and Thomas Naylor. *Affluenza: The All-Consuming Epidemic.* Second edition. San Francisco: Berrett-Koehler Publishers, 2005.

Dennison, Barbara A., Theresa J. Russo, Patrick A. Burdick, and Paul L. Jenkins. "An Intervention to Reduce Television Viewing by Preschool Children." *Archives of Pediatrics and Adolescent Medicine* 158, no. 2 (February 2004): 170–76.

Dietz, William H., and Steven L. Gortmaker. "Do We Fatten Our Children at the TV Set? Obesity and Television Viewing in Children and Adolescents." *Pediatrics* 75, no. 5 (May 1985): 807–12.

Elkind, David. *The Hurried Child.* Cambridge, MA: Perseus Publishing, 2001.

Flesher, John. "Turning Off TV Makes U.P. Kids Less Aggressive." *Lansing State Journal*, January 28, 2006.

Fox, Roy F. *Harvesting Minds: How TV Commercials Control Kids.* Westport, CT: Praeger Publishers, 1996.

Healy, Jane. *Endangered Minds: Why Children Don't Think—and What We Can Do About It.* New York: Touchstone Books, 1999.

Henry J. Kaiser Family Foundation. "The Role of Media in Childhood Obesity." Publication no. 7030. February 2004. Available at http://www.kff.org/entmedia/upload/The-Role-of-Media-in-Childhood-Obesity.pdf

Kingsolver, Barbara. "The One-Eyed Monster, and Why I Don't Let Him In." In *Small Wonders: Essays*, pp. 131–43. New York: HarperCollins, 2002.

Kubey, Robert, and Mihaly Csikszentmihalyi. "Television Addiction Is No Mere Metaphor." *Scientific American*, February 2002, pp. 74–80.

———. *Television and the Quality of Life: How Viewing Shapes Everyday Experience.* Hillsdale, NJ: Lawrence Erlbaum Associates, 1990.

Kunkel, Dale. "Children and Television Advertising." In *Handbook of Children and the Media* (new ed.), ed. Dorothy G. Singer and Jerome L. Singer, pp. 375–94. Thousand Oaks, CA: Sage Publications, 2002.

Levin, Diane E. *Remote Control Childhood? Combating the Hazards of Media Culture.* Washington, D.C.: National Association for the Education of Young Children, 1998.

Mander, Jerry. *Four Arguments for the Elimination of Television.* New York: Quill Press, 1978.

McKibben, Bill. *Enough: Staying Human in an Engineered Age.* New York: Henry Holt and Company, 2003.

McNeal, James. *The Kids' Market.* Ithaca, NY: Paramount Market Publishing, 1999.

Monczunski, John. "Spent." *Notre Dame Magazine Online*, Summer 2003. Available at http://www.nd.edu/-ndmag/su2003/monczunski.html

Nash, Jay B. *Philosophy of Recreation and Leisure.* St. Louis: Mosby, 1953. Repr. Dubuque, IA: William C. Brown, 1960.

National Science Foundation. "Children, TV, Computers and More Media: New Research Shows Pluses, Minuses." Press release no. 05-018. February 11, 2005. Available at http://www.nsf.gov/news/news_summ.jsp?cntn_id=102813&org=NSF&from=news

Pipher, Mary. "All That Glitters." Center for a New American Dream. Column no. 5. August–September 2000. Available at http://www.newdream.org/column/5.html

———. *The Middle of Everywhere*. San Diego: Harcourt Publishing, 2002.

———. *The Shelter of Each Other*. New York: G. P. Putnam's Sons, 1996.

Postman, Neil. *Amusing Ourselves to Death*. New York: Penguin Books, 1986.

Putnam, Robert. *Bowling Alone: The Collapse and Revival of American Community*. New York: Simon & Schuster, 2000.

Rideout, Victoria J., and Elizabeth Hamel. *The Media Family: Electronic Media in the Lives of Infants, Toddlers, Preschoolers, and Their Parents*. Report of the Henry J. Kaiser Family Foundation. May 2006. Available at http://www.kff.org/entmedia/7500.cfm

Rideout, Victoria J., Elizabeth A. Vandewater, and Ellen A. Wartella. *Zero to Six: Electronic Media in the Lives of Infants, Toddlers, and Preschoolers*. Report of the Henry J. Kaiser Family Foundation. Fall 2003. Available at http://www.kff.org/entmedia/3378.cfm

Roberts, Donald F., Ulla G. Foehr, and Victoria Rideout. *Generation M: Media in the Lives of 8- to 18-Year-olds*. Report of the Henry J. Kaiser Family Foundation. March 2005. Available at http://www.kff.org/entmedia/entmedia030905pkg.cfm

Robinson, John P., and Geoffrey Godbey. *Time for Life: The Surprising Ways Americans Use Their Time*. University Park, PA: Pennsylvania State University Press, 1997.

Robinson, Thomas N., Marta L. Wilde, Lisa C. Navracruz, K. Farish Haydel, and Ann Varady. "Effects of Reducing Children's Television and Video Game Use on Aggressive Behavior: A Randomized Controlled Trial." *Archives of Pediatrics and Adolescent Medicine* 155, no. 1 (January 2001): 7–23.

Rosenberg, Bernard, and David Manning White, eds. *Mass Culture: The Popular Arts in America*. Glencoe, IL: Free Press and Falcon's Wing Press, 1957.

Russell, Ruth V. *Pastimes: The Context of Contemporary Leisure*. Second edition. Champaign, IL: Sagamore Publishing, 2002.

living outside the box

Schor, Juliet. *Born to Buy: The Commercialized Child and the New Consumer Culture*. New York: Scribner, 2004.

————. *The Overworked American*. New York: Basic Books, 1992.

Senate Judiciary Staff Report, United States Congress. *Children, Violence, and the Media: A Judiciary Committee Staff Report for Parents and Policymakers*. Washington, D.C.: U. S. Government Printing Office, 1999.

Shifrin, Donald. "Effect of Media on Children and Adolescents: It's About Time." *Archives of Pediatrics and Adolescent Medicine* 160, no. 4 (April 2006): 448–50.

Singer, Dorothy G., and Jerome L. Singer. *Handbook of Children and the Media*. New edition. Thousand Oaks, CA: Sage Publications, 2002.

State of California. Department of Health Services. California Obesity Prevention Initiative. "Do More, Watch Less." Available at http://www.dhs.ca.gov/ps/cdic/copi/copiforms/tvtool.htm

State of California. Department of Health Services. *California Obesity Prevention Plan: A Vision for Tomorrow, Strategic Actions for Today*. 2006. Available at http://www.dhs.ca.gov/CAObesityPrevention/

Steyer, James P. *The Other Parent: The Inside Story of the Media's Effect on Our Children*. New York: Atria Books, 2002.

Surgeon General's Report. *Physical Activity and Health*. Centers for Disease Control and Prevention, National Center for Chronic Disease Prevention and Health Promotion, and in collaboration with the President's Council on Physical Fitness and Sports. Washington, D.C.: U.S. Government Printing Office, 1996.

Trelease, Jim. *The Read-Aloud Handbook*. New York: Penguin Books, 2001.

Wallis, Claudia. "The Multitasking Generation." *Time*, March 27, 2006, pp. 48–56.

Winn, Marie. *The Plug-In Drug*. New York: Penguin Books, 2002.

Wynne, Sharon Kennedy. "TV Fit for Kids." *St. Petersburg Times* (Tampa Bay), January 24, 2006. Available at hhtp://www/sptimes.com/2006/01/24/news_pf/Floridian/TV_fit_for_kids.shtml

Zimmerman, Frederick J., and Dimitri A. Christakis. "Children's Television Viewing and Cognitive Outcomes." *Archives of Pediatrics and Adolescent Medicine* 159, no. 7 (July 2005): 619–25.

bibliography

Zimmerman, Frederick J., Gwen M. Glew, Dimitri A. Christakis, and Wayne Katon. "Early Cognitive Stimulation, Emotional Support, and Television Watching as Predictors of Subsequent Bullying Among Grade-School Children." *Archives of Pediatrics and Adolescent Medicine* 159, no. 4 (April 2005): 384–88.

about the author

A professor of recreation management at Eastern Washington University for the past twenty years, Barbara Brock is widely known for her innovative research into TV-free life-styles. Articles about her work have appeared in *Time* magazine and in numerous other publications, including *Parenting*, *Woman's Day*, *Family Circle*, and *Good Housekeeping*. Perhaps ironically, she has also appeared on the *Today Show*, in an interview with Katie Couric. For over two decades now, she and her husband, together with their two children and a gaggle of pets, have lived very contentedly without television.